JUBILEE

JUBILEE

A MONK'S JOURNAL

M. Basil Pennington, O.C.S.O.

 PAULIST PRESS   *New York/Ramsey*

Library of Congress
Catalog Card Number: 81-82336

ISBN: 0-8091-2402-5

Published by Paulist Press
545 Island Road, Ramsey, N.J. 07446

Printed and bound in the
United States of America

Contents

TO
FATHER OWEN HOEY, O.C.S.O.
FELLOW ALUMNUS
BROTHER MONK
ESTEEMED SPIRITUAL LEADER
ON THE OCCASION OF THE
GOLDEN JUBILEE
OF HIS PROFESSION
1930—DECEMBER 10—1980

Foreword

A few years ago, after returning from a very unusual and fruitful retreat on Mount Athos, I was induced to publish the journal I kept during that time. That journal, in fact, contained three rather diverse elements. In one sense it was a travelogue, describing a most fascinating monastic republic and the daily life of its citizens. In this regard, it was rather unique, for never before had a monk of the West been allowed to enter so intimately and fully into the life of these monks. Another significant element was the ecumenical sharing and insights. For Orthodoxy, as for most of the great religions, monasticism is at the heart of the Church, of the spiritual life of its peoples. Therefore ecumenical dialogue in the monastic context and at the level of spiritual practice and experience has a primary import. The third element of the journal I considered the least significant: the reflective sharings of my own personal experience in the course of the retreat. It came to me as something of a surprise then when both reviewers and those who were moved to write to the author centered upon this third element.

We are all on a journey, the pilgrimage of the people of God. We each climb the mountain, seek the inner sanctuary, the Kingdom of God. In many ways it is a solitary journey, even in a crowd. But we are not alone before the all-holy and awesome One. We are all in this together. To express this, Merton once used as the title of a book the classic phrase: *No Man (or Woman) Is an Island.* Yet it is all too rare that a fellow pilgrim shares with us the anguish and the joy of his or her own faltering steps along the way. Because so many found the personal sharing in *O Holy Mountain* of some help, encouragement, and consolation—misery loves company, and we, each

1

in his or her own way, are miserable sinners, even while we are redeemed and much loved sharers in the Divine life—I have been encouraged to share some other jottings from my journal.

The sharing in these pages gives some intimate glimpses into Cistercian life as it is lived today—its thoughts, its concerns, its hopes. I suspect many will find them much broader and more varied, more far-reaching than they expected.

There is considerable interest in monastic life at the present time. In the midst of the increasing instability and frenetic activity of the world, men and women are drawn more and more to seek the inner cell of the heart. There is something of the monk in every person. When we come home to ourselves, it is silence and solitude.

Those whose lives are actively engaged in the struggle to bring the Lord's creation to fullness through family life and creative activity look to monks and nuns to show them how to enter into this inner cell and how to conduct themselves, once they are there.

What you have here is the expression of but one particular monk. It will undoubtedly speak more to some than to others. It does not pretend to be a complete answer to such questions as: How do you come to the Center, to the heart, to the ground of your being? What do you do when you get there? How do you find that deep inner peace and joy that will prevail even as you go out again into activity—a peace, a joy, a light that will flow into this activity? These gleanings simply share some of the thoughts (his own and borrowings) and experiences of a particular monk who has gratefully found a peace and a joy in life beyond anything he could have hoped for or imagined.

We are made to the image of God. Our happiness and our fullness lies in being like our heavenly Father. If the opening pages of our Scriptures tell us that God rested on the seventh day after six days of labor, it is to remind us of the need of restful and restorative spaces in our lives. God looked upon the fruit of his labor, saw that it was good, and sat back and enjoyed it. Later, when he deigned to choose for himself a particular people and give them a law and a way of life, he decreed for them, also, a Sabbath rest.

To this he added a Sabbath year:

> Speak to the sons of Israel and say to them: When you
> enter the land that I am giving you, the land is to keep
> a Sabbath's rest for Yahweh. For six years you shall
> sow your field, for six years you shall prune your vine
> and gather its produce. But in the seventh year the
> land is to have its rest, a Sabbath for Yahweh. You
> must not sow your field nor prune your vine, or har-
> vest your ungathered corn or gather grapes from your
> untrimmed vine. It is to be a year of rest for the land.
> The Sabbath of the land will itself feed you and your
> servants, men and women, your hired laborer, your
> guest, and all who live with you. For your cattle too,
> and the animals on your land, all its produce will serve
> as food. (Lev. 25:2–7)

This is a practice which some professions—all too few—
continue to respect. It is a need of every human person, most
especially those who have as their ministry to bring the saving
and healing presence of the Lord to his people. How priests
and religious can expect to be able to minister fruitfully year
in and year out without any respite or spaces for contemplation and renewal, I do not understand. Their own lives should
teach the rhythm and the ways of the Lord.

Over and above the Sabbath year, the Lord added the
year of Jubilee—the fiftieth year added on to the seventh
Sabbath year, as a special time of grace and respite:

> You are to count seven weeks of years—seven times
> seven years, that is to say, a period of seven weeks of
> years, forty-nine years. And on the tenth day of the
> seventh month you shall sound the trumpet; on the
> Day of Atonement you shall sound the trumpet
> throughout the land. You will declare this fiftieth year
> sacred and proclaim the liberation of all the inhabit-
> ants of the land. This is to be a jubilee for you; each of
> you will return to his ancestral home, each to his own
> clan. This fiftieth year is to be a jubilee for you: you

will not sow, you will not harvest the ungathered
corn, you will not gather from the untrimmed vine.
The jubilee is to be a holy thing to you; you will eat
what comes from the fields. (Lev. 25:8–13)

Traditionally, the Year of Jubilee has been seen as symbol-
ic of the contemplative life. It is the contemplatives' joy and
grace and privilege—and responsibility—to step out of the
regular rhythm of life, and live a life of repose before the Lord,
to leave off the normal productive activity of men and women,
and lie fallow, letting their fruitfulness come from the Lord
himself.

By God's design, all were to be nourished freely from the
fruitfulness he himself gave to the Sabbath rest, the Jubilee
Year:

For six years you may sow your land and gather its
produce, but in the seventh year you must let it lie
fallow and forego all produce from it. Those of your
people who are poor may take food from it, and let
the wild animals feed on what they leave. You shall do
the same with your vineyard and your olive grove.
(Ex. 23:10–11)

And so it is that the fruits which the Lord raises up in the
contemplative heart and within the contemplative community
are in fact for all his people, for whoever would care to come
and glean them.

This year at Spencer Abbey we are celebrating a particular Jubilee—the Golden Jubilee of Father Owen Hoey. When
Father Owen came to the community in 1928, the life was in
many outward respects quite different, though essentially the
same. The existence of the small community in Valley Falls,
Rhode Island, which farmed the rocky New England soil,
picked apples, and gathered eggs, was marked with a greater
poverty and austerity than today's community. I do not know
many of the details of Father's life. I am sure some of the older
Fathers could fill in the story with many colorful anecdotes.
Father was soon ordained to the priesthood and asked to teach,
and to serve as a superior. Through the many years that

followed he was Abbot Edmund Futterer's great support, both as his immediate assistant and as novice master. Father Owen was sent in 1950 as founding superior of the Abbey of Our Lady of the Holy Cross in Berryville, Virginia. In 1952 Dom Edmund recalled him to be Prior of the newly founded Abbey at Spencer, where he served until he was sent forth again in 1959, this time as founding father of the first Trappist monastery in South America. It was not easy for an elderly man to learn a new language and adapt to a new culture.

Solid foundations were laid for a new flourishing community. And again Father Owen was summoned back to Spencer, to assist a new young Abbot, Dom Thomas Keating, as his Prior. When Father was finally relieved of this service, Abbot Thomas constituted him dean, a largely honorary office, with a special stall in choir—an institutional expression, we might say, of the very special presence that Father Owen is in the midst of the community.

This volume offers some of the pickings of a Year of Jubilee—not the fruits of systematically cultivated thought, but random outcroppings, free to all who would care to sample them. They were gleaned in the hope that they might in some little way nourish the poor of spirit, my fellow citizens in the Kingdom. They do not in fact all come from the same year, for I do not tend ordinarily to write that frequently in my journal. But for a contemplative, every year is Jubilee. Our year is not divided into months—named in part after pagan gods—but into seasons of grace. We Christians live a cycle that is our own in Christ. We have been baptized into Christ. "I live, now not I, but Christ lives in me." (Gal. 2:20) We live the life of Christ, our head. We live Salvation History. Each year for us is to live again with Christ his many saving mysteries, to live again the journey of a chosen people going out from the bondage of Egyptian worldliness (no reference to today's Egypt, but to the Biblical type) through the saving waters of the Red Sea, baptismal renewal, the desert experience and the encounter with God and his law, till Joshua—Jesus, our savior and leader— brings us safely into the Promised Land. Our year then is Advent and Christmas, Lent, Resurrection and Ascension, Pentecost, Dedication and Pilgrimage, till we come to the glorious reign of our King and our God, in our hearts, among our people, in our world, and in the fullness of all times and peoples. When we are living at this level of awareness, our life is immensely exciting even if at the level of appearances it is the fallow time of Jubilee. We may not have spectacular things to write or share, but something wonderful is going on as a life-giving soil becomes yet richer and more vital, a vitality of which perhaps the spontaneous random outcroppings give some hint.

I will be very happy if this sharing invites you to get a little more in touch with the wonderful things that are actually going on in your life as a person tenderly and eternally loved and affirmed by the Lord—a person whose each day is in fact an unfolding of Salvation History and the life of Christ among his people. When we are in touch with the true dimensions of who we are and what is actually going on in our apparently fallow lives, we can only acclaim with the Psalmist: "I thank you, God, for the wonder of my being."

And let me thank, here, not only my God whom I can never thank enough, but all those who by his grace so constantly nourish my life and being. The many ways in which Father Owen has been a benediction to me are beyond description: presence, affirming love, example, encouragement, ceaseless intercession before the Face of the Lord, guidance, compassion, consolation, and so much more. And he is just one—a most special and outstanding one—of a whole community of brethren and scores and scores of loved ones and friends scattered across this earth and into the heavenly Kingdom. To all of them, thanks! I will add a special word of thanks to that most dear little Sister whose typing fingers and praying heart make it possible for my random thoughts to be gathered into readable pages. May the Lord himself be her reward.

Fr. Basil

Feast of the Immaculate Conception
December 8, 1980
at Spencer Abbey

HE COMES!

First Sunday of Advent

Rorate coeli desuper—Drop down dew, ye heavens, from above.

The first candle of the Advent wreath is lit. The monastery resounds with the first longing cries of Advent: Drop down dew, you heavens. . . . Come, Lord Jesus, come! With longing do we long. The liturgical mystery responds so completely to the reality. Advent is a glorious season, so full of hope—hope that touches the deepest chords within our hearts. The longing for a Savior, for a healer, for love, for life. In these coming days may my whole being be a "Come, Lord Jesus, come!"

*   *   *

This morning as I dressed, a practice from my childhood days flashed into my mind. I think it was Sister Emily who started us on it in the fourth grade. We were to prepare a place for Jesus in our hearts. So many Masses made a gold bedstead; so many Communions, a fluffy down mattress. Other practices produced sheets, blankets, pillows, etc. The central thing—and I forget what it did—was to pray four thousand times—once for each year Adam's sons had waited—the prayer: "Jesus, Son of Mary, come and take birth in my heart." Thus Advent became for us a time of constant prayer. I don't know if Sister realized she was introducing us to an ancient prayer practice, one with the Jesus Prayer.

I wonder if Sister Emily still prepares a Christmas crib in her heart . . . I do.

*   *   *

I have received a book to review (in fact, two different magazines have sent me the same book) with essays on "Creation-centered Spirituality." An angry young man—or so he seems—writes the introduction, lashing out at all the evils of

9

"fall/redemption-spirituality." I for one am quite ready to admit that there was a fall, and I have done some falling of my own. So I am very happy that there is a redemption, that I have been redeemed. That is what Advent is all about—the coming of a *Redeemer.* "You shall conceive and bear a son and his name will be called *Jesus,* because he will save his people from their sins." Alleluia! (I am glad they have not suppressed that during Advent.)

*   *   *

The angel spoke to Joseph about *Jesus* meaning *savior* and saving from sin. With more delicacy he spoke to Mary about greatness, about a throne and an everlasting reign. Maybe this is "creation spirituality." Both are true. Both have their place. We need both: to be picked up from our sinful fallen state and to rise to reign with him, the master of creation. We are priests who give creation a voice in the liturgy of our labor and our love—for it, too, groans for redemption in and through and with us.

*   *   *

Feast of St. Ambrose

"Ambrose for bishop!"—no matter that he was a civil magistrate. No matter that he was not yet baptized. He was the best Christian leader around, catechumen though he was. How good it will be when we return to the time when the people choose their bishops, when the best Christian leaders available are chosen to lead the Christian community, other considerations being set aside. Then bishops will again be saints.

*   *   *

Second Sunday of Advent

John sacrificed all other joys so that he might have the joy of welcoming the Lord. He had a foretaste of this in the womb.

Then he leapt for joy at the Lord's presence. But it was a wiser, deeper man, tempered by the desert, who welcomed the Lord at the Jordan with humble sobriety. All of this is at the heart of monastic life. Oftentimes in the nascent days of monastic conversion there is that exultant ecstatic encounter with the Lord that causes one to bound with joy. But then come the long desert years, the school of humility—which is at the center of Saint Benedict's Rule—constantly looking toward and finding meaning in that coming of the Lord—that "visit of the Word," as Saint Bernard calls it. If we are faithful he will come, and come again, until, in response to our heartfelt plea, "Master, where do you dwell?" he responds, "Come and see," and we pass with him into the blissful state of constant union. Before that is fully achieved we may, like John, have to experience darkness and imprisonment and even in some way "lose our heads."

*   *   *

Like John, we have to lose our heads for Christ.

We may have the great privilege of doing this literally. I just read the account of our monks in China who had their heads crushed with stones by the Communists after months of torture and dehumanizing treatment of all sorts.

But there is another way in which we all can and must lose our heads. We must in some way let go of our conceptual and logical dominance and let our hearts take over. As Saint Thomas Aquinas said—and experienced on Saint Nicholas day in 1273—the heart can go beyond where the head has to leave off. From those realms we well know, as Thomas did, that all our finest reasoning—even the most lofty speculations of theology, the whole of the *Summa Theologica*—are all just so much straw in comparison with the experience of the Lord. When we come to experience this, then, for us, as for Saint Thomas and our Father Saint Bernard, the breathing of love, the Song of Songs, will be what makes most sense.

*

Reason unaided by love can lead us only to pride.

*

Clarity is not enough, but irrationality won't do.

*

God gave us our faculties to work with ... they must be allowed to perform their office until God gives them a better one.

*

They are eminently reasonable folks; their love is not yet ardent enough to overwhelm their reason.
                                        ——Saint Teresa of Avila

*   *   *

"What did you go out to the desert to seek?"

The Lord asks each one of us. And we must ask ourselves. "A shaking reed?" Yes, in a way, for we seek self-knowledge and find that we are shaky reeds. We might have discovered that at home—if we had just found enough quiet to get in touch with ourselves. But no—we do not want to spend our whole time contemplating our shaky selves, nor the shakiness—the faults, failures, or weaknesses of ourselves or our fellows.

"Men in soft garments?"—a luxurious life. We can be seeking the consolations of God instead of God himself in our desert experience. The pleasure principle is profoundly deep in us.

"A prophet?" Yes—one greater than John: one who not only knows the Lord Jesus but has been baptized into him and transformed in him. One who knows the way to all that our hearts desire, one who is one with the Way and makes him present. We need the desert, the silent time apart, and we need the prophet, the spiritual guide, the spiritual father. We have come into the desert to seek God. Sinai and then the

Promised Land is our goal. Come, Lord Jesus, come, and show us the way, for you are the Way.

*

He is a fool who trusts his own wit; follow the rule of wise men, if you would reach safety.

——Proverbs 28:26

* * *

My life has sort of moved along in cycles through the years following the first years of contemplative freedom—although even from the start I had various charges in the abbey: sacristy, choir books, a period on construction and on foundation. Then came the *theology* phase—1957–1961: preparation for Rome, a year in Rome, two years of teaching; the *Canon Law* phase, 1961–1969: two years in Rome, teaching, Canon Law Society, Consilium Monasticum Iuris Canonici, work on the Code, writing; the *Cistercian Studies* phase, 1969–1973: Cistercian Publications, Symposia, Institute of Cistercian Studies, writing, editing; *Orthodox relations*, 1973–1977: the third Symposium, trip to Byzantium, Israel; retreat on Mount Athos, books; *Centering Prayer*, 1974–1979: Conference of Major Superiors, workshops, books, and tapes; *vocation ministry*, 1978–: vocation director, ERVDA, writing, tapes. Now, along with vocations, the *East-West relations*, which started with Yoga, Zen, Ramakrishna contacts, and the Petersham meeting, to continue with the coming trip to India. Out of all this, a global consciousness is rising. Is this to be the emerging cycle?

*

And then I will pour cleansing streams over you, to purge you from every stain you bear, purge you from the taint of your idolatry. (How easily I can make idols of what I do.) I will give you a new heart, and breathe a new spirit into you; so shall you make your home in the land I promised to your fathers . . . And there will be a new heaven and a new earth. . . .

*   *   *

The stirring of the Spirit is deep. There is a widespread materialism and selfishness grasping at the American heart, yet there are magnificent youth, refinding the Gospel and Christ and wanting to be total in whatever way they walk. The vocation ministry today is inspiring, challenging, uplifting, but exhausting. There are far too few in it with a sufficiently catholic vision, both as to breadth and depth. Too often the vision is too shallow, divorced from the richness of our tradition, and too sectarian, lacking the ecumenical and transcultural openness of Vatican II. So I put a certain amount of me into ministering to the ministers, a good bit into the youth who come—some not so young, but young in the Lord—and try yet to be anchored deep and live out of the center where God and I are more one than even a pantheist can express.

*   *   *

As a man gives way to grace, a number of natural phenomena follow from the action of the grace. In vocational discernment, the question that must come first is not what is happening on the phenomenological level, but what is behind it, what are the feelings in the depths. The phenomena are ambivalent.

For too long we had been emphasizing too exclusively the action of the Spirit and not considering sufficiently the psychological laws that can govern these phenomena. We must do this without losing any of the sacred involved. The pendulum has swung.

At the moment, many directors are tending to approach only from the natural psychological approach. This is one of the dangers of psychological screening. It can take over the supernatural. There needs to be interdisciplinary cooperation. True spiritual experience and appreciation for the sacred needs to be linked with current human knowledge.

The aim of direction should be to make the candidate

aware at all levels how to use the means, while inserting them fully into an awareness of grace and an habitual attitude of receptivity to grace. For this there should be true poverty of spirit and great dependence on the Spirit. Data must be interpreted in the light of the spiritual.

*

Our meeting with God cannot come about only through the natural world and man. There must be immediate contact with God in the depths of our consciences. There must be a direct I-Thou experience, a mystical experience. Not everything can be reduced to the natural. In the quest for God we use both natural and mystical.

*

The candidate should be truly seeking God, and not just seeking his own fulfillment. However, a Spiritual Father has to meet the man where he is. If he is seeking self-fulfillment, by loving him, by kindness, we can draw him out to true love and lead him on to true outgoing love of his fellow human being, and of God. In the past this was not so necessary, for the young man came seeking God, but today it is necessary.

*

In responding to others, we must be conscious of responding to God in them. But we do not always need others to respond to God. We need to enter into solitude where we can respond to God in himself.

With regard to interpersonal relations, the Trappist ideal has been too rigid. It has been too affected by the achieving attitude (achieving one's holiness). It has not been responsive enough to natural human qualities. But the contemplative way of life necessarily puts God psychologically in the center of things.

*

The way chosen by the contemplative will affect the whole Church. For here is the stronghold of the transcendent. The sense of and response to the transcendent must be preserved while renewing and casting out the obsolete. The psychological must not be used as an instrument against the transcendental. If the horizontal is allowed to take preference to the vertical, the contemplative vocation is lost. We must develop openness to the interpersonal without detracting from the vertical.

*

With regard to authenticity, if one insists on wholly authentic forms (i.e., forms which here and now express just what I feel or think) from the start, then there would be no possibility to develop. We need to enter into forms and be formed to greater things. At first there can be, and ordinarily should be, a certain appeal, but there must come a period of dryness. If I faithfully come through, I will discover myself in the forms and will express myself through them. We can renew the contemplative life only if this is accepted.

*

Questions that need further development:
- Liturgy as being truly a community communication in God.
- The Role of the Rule
  —an external norm; self-responsibility and self-determination do not require a structureless community
  —as God's will, confirming that God is here before a human person.
- *Animus-anima*—the fear of men concerning their masculinity makes them reluctant to allow the *anima* to evolve, to accept the passive role necessary in contemplation.

*   *   *

The bell rings in the distance.
The dog barks.
The Lord speaks in the heart.

*

Listen! That is the message of these Advent days. Listen, not so much with the ears or the mind, but with the heart. This means stepping back a little from our daily doings, so we can really hear what is going on, what God is doing right now in Salvation History. It means turning off the interior dialogue—that constant chatter we keep going within ourselves, mind and memory and feelings, each insisting on saying its piece—so that we can hear the still small voice that murmurs like a gentle breeze and can be heard only in the sound of silence.

Speak, Lord, your servant *wants* to hear.

*

I will lead him into the desert and there I will speak to his heart.

*

But if, when you are present in thus doing good to me, I am absent from you in mind and heart, the operations of your grace, it seems to me, are like burial rites, duly and carefully fulfilled upon a corpse.

*

Grant to those who think and speak and write of you a balanced judgment, an utterance concise and disciplined, and a heart aflame to find you, Jesus, in the Scriptures that speak concerning you.

——William of Saint Thierry

*   *   *

There is a pain, a terrible pain in my heart. I see something of the immense potential of the Catholic way to bring vitality, meaning, excitement, fullness to human life—something of the roar of the hurricane of the Spirit—and yet the actual enthusiasm or lack of it that prevails. How can we not make our own the Advent cry: "Lord, rouse up your might and come!" Our Church in America, like our nation, is so miserably lacking in great, inspired and inspiring leadership.

A hungry, searching generation turns to the Church and finds bishops and priests too preoccupied with administration and the things of this world to hear them, to be with them, to be spiritual fathers, to pray with them in a personal way, apart from the shield of ritual. Lord, give us true shepherds who will feed the flock—take little ones into their arms and tenderly care rather than act like executives of agribusiness, remote from their caged or herded animals. Isn't it time to let the more qualified laymen and women take over the administration, to let the married deacons function, and let the successors of the Apostles give themselves to prayer and teaching and healing? Lord, renew your Church, beginning with me and this community, with our diocese and our nation. Come, Lord Jesus, come!

*   *   *

The contemplative's first service to his brothers and sisters lies in the gift of his whole life, paying his and their debt to God and Maker by unceasing prayer, praise, and homage, by a living that is giving in love. To this all else is secondary.

*

The meaning of prayer lies in ever striving after an expressly new actuation of an interior attitude towards God which is suitable for us, an attitude which must not be restricted to the time of prayer alone, but which should penetrate and transform our whole life.
——Emerick Corett

*

In what way can the monk be said to be representing the Church in his prayer?

In every society it is necessary that different aspects of its life and values be made present by different members in different ways. Within the Church, prayer has to be expressed and lived in a more external way by some members because of the social nature of the Church.

We might draw a parallel with the artist. He depicts what we all can see. I share in his vision and feel myself expressed in his work. This makes me happy. If he were not there or did not do his work, I would suffer a real loss. My life experience would in some way be diminished. By his work, with his special dedication and mastery, he lifts up my vision to new levels of fullness. This is proportionately true for all the values of a society. The social body needs some who are expressing each of its particular values in a special way, even though all the members of the society are expressing and living them in some way.

If there were not monks and nuns, men and women living out the prayer dimension of the life of the Church with a special dedication and fullness, the whole society of the Church would suffer a loss, a diminution of the sacred in her life and experience. The monks and nuns represent the Church in their prayer because of the stress they place on the prayer life. The Church body is more praying there—the Church, that is, all Christians, for the monk, no matter how solitary, never prays alone. The member never prays without the body.

*

There is nothing more powerful than a man praying well.

——Saint John Chrysostom

*

A very little of this love is more precious in the sight of God and the soul—and of greater profit to the

Church, even though the soul appears to do nothing—
than are all those works together.

—Saint John of the Cross

*   *   *

Feast of Our Lady of Guadalupe

"I am a merciful Mother."

How much we need a merciful mother in our difficult
time!

Personally, my recent oral surgery prevents me from eating and leaves me uncomfortable, to say the very least. Then
there is the bursitis, the arthritis, and a chest cold. More
deeply, there is the heartache over Jim—the guilt-feeling of
having failed because of my pushing ahead too much, and not
giving enough time for reflection and prayer. Had I but followed my first instinct, it could perhaps have led to a happier
and fuller life for Jim. I will always carry him in my heart and
beg the Lord to make up for my failure. I am learning the hard
way, but it is all the more sad when it is others who pay the
biggest part of the price.

Yes, I feel my personal aches and pains. But then I lift up
my eyes and open my heart and quickly realize how little are
my sorrows, even in their poignant realness, compared to
those of so many others. I enter into the Heart of Mary, the
merciful Mother, and encounter them all: the loneliness, the
frustration, the searching, the meaninglessness, that plague so
many lives. The terrible relentless suffering and pain that
mark so many of my brothers and sisters with the Passion of
Christ—even though most do not realize this deeper and con-
soling meaning of their agony. I can hardly begin to experience and be with, not to speak of expressing, the burdens, the
sufferings, the miseries of brothers and sisters in the prison
camps of Siberia and elsewhere; in the refugee camps and
villages of Southeast Asia; the boat people (how quickly we
forget them as our interest and curiosity shift elsewhere); in
the hearts of the mothers of Belfast, among the people of
Lebanon and Palestine, El Salvador, and in all the barrios of

Latin America, through the ghettos and slums of the world—
the litany of lamentation is without end.

Yes, we, the children of the earth, need a merciful Mother
to press us to her bosom, to wipe away our tears, to be our life,
our sweetness, and our hope in this land of exile where we
have all too many reasons for mourning and weeping.

*

The risen Christ is still nailed into the sufferings of
humanity.

*   *   *

Third Sunday of Advent

On that day the ears of death shall hear the words of
the book.

——Isaiah 19

When the Lord visits us in our reading, suddenly we hear,
we see. Things we have read many times before now stand
naked, open, illumined. We see. We hear. "On that day ..."
Without this visit of the Lord, even the Scriptures are often
just so many words, hardly stirring memories. We have heard
it all before. "On that day ..." the Scriptures are fire. It is
Tabor. It is the road to Emmaus. Advent is not a longing for
some lost historical coming—not even its renewal—it is a longing for "that day." Come, Lord Jesus, come!

*

Be patient, brothers, until the Lord's coming.... Do
not lose heart, because the Lord's coming will be
soon.

——James 5:7f

*

For your example take the prophets who spoke in the name of the Lord.

—Ibid.

*

If we were to get in touch with a child in the womb as it neared birth we would find the little one very comfortable, cozy, warm, set. Then as the birth process begins, the child experiences great fear; it does not want to leave its known and caring environment. But after the trauma of birth, the little one quickly feels the caress of caring hands and sees a loving, smiling face it will come to truly love. It will be nurtured and opened out to a beautiful life. It will come to love this new life . . .

But, again, there comes the time when a new transition presses upon this person. Again there is fear at leaving the known and loved. Yet, after the trauma we call death, which is really another birth, we find old familiar faces to greet us, the loving hands of our Father to caress us, and a divine smile to warm our hearts as we enter into that life which will know no end, but will be eternal. Death is but a rebirth. Life is not ended, but changed. Dying, we live forever.

*   *   *

By faith—because it is a free human act not compelled by evidence—we can say to God as he has said to us: "I want you to be, because I have loved you." Thus Mary could say, "My soul magnifies the Lord"—because she so totally believed.

EMMANUEL

God with Us

Christmas Eve

I think much of Mary today, and of pregnant mothers everywhere. They more than any can enter into the mystery which we relive now in sacramental reality. The hour approaches and life quickens. Soon an adoring (quite literally) father will be bending over the tiniest of faces, caught up in the wonder of such little ears being so finely formed, feeling the first tentative grasp of little fingers around his own great finger. The reality and the wonder of incarnation—for this is truly God, the Creator of all. The gentleness of our God, to reach to us like this! If we can really touch him here, we will not miss him in the rest of his creation; all will be shot through with incarnation.

We recoil from pantheism. We know our God personally. He is a loving Father and not some ingredient of all that is. And yet, we perhaps recoil too far and miss the reality of his loving creative presence in all. The very tiny Infant, a few pounds of life, wrapped up, a Christmas gift to us all, is a challenge. Perhaps we have become too used to the crib scene to sense how it insults our reason and calls down all our pride, for we are to adore and acknowledge complete and total dependence on such manifest impotence and dependence.

If we can really become alive to the divine here, we will readily behold the divine in all, and our life will become one of humble adoration, and constant prayer, immense joy. The closeness, the care, the gentleness, the wonder, the love of our God. *Our* God, yes, ours, because this day he comes as purest gift. We have but to receive. And to be sure we are not frightened away, the gift comes to us in the hands of a sweet young mother, one of the disenfranchised poor.

O holy Mother, take out of my heart all fear. Show me how to hold your little One, to hold him in my heart.

Joseph, courageous father, teach me something of your virile gentleness.

*　　*　　*

Christmas

Emmanuel—God with us.

Christ is born again in our world. And it is only the scattered few outside the mainstream of man's rush for wealth and power who watch in the night and receive the good news. But he comes for all, to bring peace to those who would have it. Good will is the condition for peace. And that is what is so sadly lacking on the international scene—and the national and local scene, too, in many cases. We do not wish our fellow human beings well. We see the world as a diminishing cake and seek to get the biggest piece we can for ourselves, with little care for our fellows.

The Lord comes as a gift of love, and the good news he brings is a message of love. He does not come to nullify any of the good of the past, but to bring it to fullness. His one new command is the way to peace, to fullness: Love as I have loved. This is good will, the essential good will: to love as God loves—he who sets his sun to shine on the good and bad alike, who lets his rain fall upon us all—his rain of grace. The heavens have dropped down their Dew. We have salvation and the way to peace. Yet so few hear the message this night. Few are listening. Angel choirs sing in vain. We are too full of our greedy compulsive activity to hear and learn the way to what we claim to seek—global peace. Certainly, our own poor hearts cry out for peace. But everything about us leads us away from it: the false standards and values of this world, the peer pressures, the compulsions of our own passions, all the forces that play on our emotions. How desperately we need to go apart from the noisy crowd and to watch in the quiet of the night so that we may hear the good news which will find an echo in the deepest places of our own hearts. We do have a Savior and in him we have a way to peace.

*

I used to smile when people asked, "What time is Midnight Mass?" Now I wait for their startled reactions when I answer: "Around 4:00 A.M." We rose at 2:00 A.M. and began the Vigil at 2:30. It lasted about an hour, certainly nothing of the fullness of the old Latin Vigils with their culminating twelfth responsory: *Et Verbum caro factum est.* But the Office had its own beauty and richness. Then the younger brethren sang their carols and played their instruments while we prepared for the pontifical Mass. We had moved the Mass from midnight to reduce the crowds of visitors, and it proved rather effective. The church was still full, but people were not standing in the aisles or out on the porch. As the Liturgy proceeded and all the bells rang out to proclaim the birth of the King, our Lord, we could easily forget that the night was not exactly in the middle of its course. That sacred moment of Salvation History when God appeared on earth as man—a squalling infant with an almost infinite need of our love and care—was again present.

Welcome, Lord Jesus! We fail for so great a part to be aware of your presence in our lives. But may your saving presence never fail us. May it ever be the healing, enlivening soul of all we think and do, bringing our whole being into harmony and peace, into perfect union with you, your Father and the Holy Spirit of Love.

*   *   *

New Year's Day

Thank God for another year of life!

The past year has been filled with many graces and blessings and plans that carry over into this year and which I humbly hope will lead to greater freedom and deeper renewal by the end of the year. I fear, though, to make too many plans, lest I in some way cop out from a complete and decisive surrender to Jesus *now.*

I have made some small resolves to try to offset some of my weaknesses so evident in this past year:

I will get in at least one or two hours of mental prayer each day, and one or two hours of *lectio.*

I will say every hour of the Office, even when dispensed or excused.

I will try to write daily in a journal.

I will do daily exercise, not eat between meals, and get out for some fresh air.

But the heart of the problem is self-will. If I did not have to take any initiative, I would be O.K. But where I meet my struggle is where I take initiative. Then I am loath to submit. There are things I want to do and plan to do, and I don't want to submit them to authority lest I get a "no."

Lord Jesus, have mercy on me and convert me to total love.

*

Do not trust too much in your present dispositions. Nothing is so fixed in the soul as not to decay with neglect and time.

——Saint Bernard

*

What does the year hold?
- *Physically:* some pain, a hospital trip this Thursday, surgery on the 16th. But on the whole I am in fairly good shape, thank God.
- *Workwise:* more and more men to work for and with. I need time for quietness with the Lord to keep on top of it and to get enough rest. Today I was very tired and slept extra in the afternoon.
- *Writing commitments:* more than a half dozen waiting on my desk.
- *Travels:* six or seven trips lined up for this year.

And the whole wonderful adventure of a life of love, each day uncovering new glimpses, new vistas, entering into new experiences.

In all I feel free, needy but content, fearful of the contentment, a sinner, unfaithful in so many ways. Lord, help! Mary, take this year. Joseph, be with us. Benedict, help us to be as we ought.

*

I preached this morning on Mary, our Mother, how she wants us to be like her—ever pondering in our hearts the good things that God has done for us.

*

I will begin to prepare to get as much as possible out of the retreat that we are to have in February. Up to now I have in many respects short-changed the Lord in living out my monastic commitment. I will—if he will only give me the grace—try to begin to live it wholly. I should begin today. But I know that to really respond to what a monk should be I need all the help I can get—the regular life and lots of time for prayer, reflection, and reading. I will try to live in his presence and beg for the grace that he will compel my rebellious will to do his totally.

God has been very good to me in the past year in spite of my own unfaithfulness to a truly contemplative way. He has taught me much. Now I must live it. With Mary's help, for I belong to her. I renew the vow by which I gave myself completely to her in 1950.

*

Of late I have found a few little books that have been very helpful: Diffenbach: *Ordinary Mystical Prayer*—in a simple, precise way, it gave me insight into what God was doing in me; Blosius, *Mirror for Monks*—made me see more clearly what I could do and be; *Un intinere de la retour a Dieu*—a good introduction by Gilson briefly outlining Saint Bernard's mystical theology, helping me to see that I do need to study more myself, my human nature, to know myself that I might know God, might seek him, return to him.

*   *   *

I am very tired today. I spent three hours this morning with three friars from a neighboring monastery who are in crisis. I tried to pass on what little I have. I am grateful for the opportunity to help others but sometimes I wonder if I am not very superficial or even hollow. Certainly to a greater extent than most suspect. Lord, have mercy, and make up for all my deficiencies.

*   *   *

I failed today in watching my food intake.

I think of my failures first. Why? Should I not first bless God for my successes? I encourage affirmation. I could begin with God and myself. I think it would be good, in this journal, as a sort of *starchestvo*, to record each day the word the Lord gives me, and then what happens in the light of this word.

*

Noah obeyed God when he took up his hammer and saw.

*

Feeling tired, dull, yet peaceful, content. Praise God!

*   *   *

When I woke up this morning I kissed the icon of Christ and thanked him for making me his disciple. He said: "Learn of me for I am *meek* and humble of heart and you will find *rest* for your soul." And added, "Blessed are the meek for theirs is the kingdom of heaven." I will take meekness as a further theme for this year.

*

I went down to the House of Affirmation to investigate a practicum for vocation directors. I see the value of working with a peer group, but at the same time I experience a certain fear of the vulnerability in such openness with a peer group. I think though it will be worth pursuing.

*   *   *

Feast of the Epiphany

The Magi made it! They never heard the Master say: "Seek and you shall find," but they sought and they found. A curious, long search. What kept them going? What keeps us going? An inner word has been spoken to us in our hearts—whether it be through a star or our own particular media. Sometime, somehow, the way, certain yet unclear, has been pointed out to us with the assurance that at its end we will find our hearts' desire—the King of our hearts. And so we stumble along—lucky if we can find some companions who have seen the same star, received the same message, seek the same King. And there are guides who do know the way—the Churchmen with the Revelation—even if that surest of messages has not spoken to their own hearts and they are set on other courses or none at all. They sit on the chair of the Master. We must do what they say if we are to follow the way—but ofttimes we cannot do what they do.

*

Perseverance—that's the note that marked the journey of the wise men—and hope. Certainly it is hard to keep going—really keep going when the vision is not constant or the sign is not all that clear. Probably the Magi's greatest help was that they were not alone. They confirmed each other in their belief, their hope—that the sign was really seen, that it was understood and true, even though all the world around them seemed oblivious of it and took them for visionaries, fools chasing after a star. They believed, they hoped, and they kept going. What do I believe, what do I hope, with whom do I share my visions, do I keep going?

*   *   *

Even the just man falls seven times a day. We need, in a way, to be comfortable with ourselves as sinners. What can you expect from a sinner but sin? Christ came for sinners—not the just (who really don't exist except in their own minds). If we really love him we can be happy in his having the glory of being our Savior.

*   *   *

Loneliness is a testing.

*   *   *

In acquiring salvation no one should be closer to you as a brother than the only son of your mother.

——Saint Bernard

*   *   *

For Yahweh says this:

To the eunuchs who observe my sabbaths and are resolved to do what pleases me and cling to my covenant, I will give, in my house and within my walls, a monument and a name, better than sons and daughters; I will give them an everlasting name that shall never be effaced.

——Isaiah 56:4f

Everything in life that is accepted undergoes a change.

*   *   *

When God blesses, it is a new creation and I am made more lovable.

*   *   *

Once I acknowledge your lovability I allow your personality to emerge.

*   *   *

Women find God in little things—in little bits they take their
solitude; men take their solitude in gulps.

*   *   *

Women generally encourage men to develop their female
side, but men do not equally encourage women to develop
their male side. They experience that as competitive.

*   *   *

The fact that God is first reaching for us makes all Christian
prayer different.

*   *   *

We look at history backwards, and it seems capricious.
                              ——John Calvin

*   *   *

Brother Albert and I went to Holy Transfiguration for the
Solemn Vespers of Saint Basil. During the early part of the
office Jesus was very present to me in the ikon on the ikonosta-
sis and spoke to my heart. It was a real visit, with the grace of
conversion. After the temptations and failures of a week of
trial, I think it will be one of those moments of lasting significance in my life.

*

I praise and bless you, Lord Jesus. Help me to begin anew
quietly and simply.

*   *   *

I feel very tired because I feel very pushed. The daily demands are absorbing all my time and there are many things hanging over my head—things I want to get done but don't see how I can get them done in time. A couple of times today a sense of relief came as I prayed: "Thy will be done," especially at the "Our Father" of the early Mass. I need to breathe more deeply and stay at that level as I quietly go about the task of the moment.

*

I read some of the *Orthodox Word* today. It is beautiful and inspiring. I need more and more of the Eastern Fathers.

*

I received a note from a nun telling of an inspiring dream she had recently in which I appeared, harking back to a conference I gave a couple of years ago. I must confess it rather pleased me. Is that pure vanity? I will have to ask the Abbot about it when I see him tomorrow. But I thank God for any good that comes to Sister or anyone else from the sharing I am asked to do.

*   *   *

Everyone said he was crazy. To be a true follower of Christ, do we not need to be a bit—at least—crazy in the eyes and according to the standards of this world? I think so.

We must, as Christ's disciples, don the slave's apron—and actually serve. Father Aquinas preached a good homily on this. The Abbot spoke in chapter on living out of faith, which means letting go of our own norms of what is good, right and desirable, and accepting what God sends our way.

The community is struggling with colds, etc., and so am I. I haven't been going to the Offices. At least it has given me an opportunity to catch up on the mail, some thirty or forty letters going out in the morning. It is rainy and cold.

*   *   *

Retreat Day

It was too cold to stay at the hermitage so I stayed in my room. It worked out fairly well. I have a bit of a head cold, so I am not too clear. I am experiencing a lot of anguish because of the increasing realization of my very real limitations in every respect—as a person, a Christian, a monk. I need to accept these limitations fully and peacefully in every way. Reverend Father, in speaking to me Thursday, pointed out how this touches on the mystery of predestination. I must fully accept my role in the Mystical Body and in the community and try to set aside, ignore, and overcome the deep-rooted desires I have to be somebody—popular, loved, of service, appreciated, esteemed—and accept being just another monk. My fulfillment has to be found in a deep personal union and love of Jesus, sharing with him, in the way he chooses and daily indicates, his work of saving the world. I will try to live this more fully by giving more time to reading the Gospels—to get to know him and his mind—and to prayer. It is the inner calm, quiet, constant, total response to Christ that matters. I must especially try to be gentle in my response to the brethren and to all situations. With all my heart I renew my vows and my special vow of belonging wholly to Mary.

*　　　*　　　*

I have been reading the Song of Songs. How the Lord seeks us! But we are settled in our lazy ways and slow to respond. I have been quite lazy today, nursing this cold. I have done little real *lectio*, but got the manuscript of *In Search of True Wisdom* copyedited and sent off; also a couple of articles.

*　　　*　　　*

I didn't really keep a gospel word today. In general I have been hazy—blame it on acedia or just a cold that lingers in my chest. I started a chapter of my new book, but didn't get very far.

*

I feel badly about George, the priest who has been here about four weeks and who is leaving the priesthood. I have not really related with him. I don't think he really wanted any relation. It is difficult to say why he came—maybe to satisfy others or some inner urge, but I think he was pretty well set before coming. He has worked generously and cooperatively. May God be with him and bless him. The negativity that goes out to a man when he leaves the priesthood certainly does not make it easy for him to get through the crisis period without growing bitter and becoming alienated from the church community. How much we all need to grow in Christ's compassion! The reasons that lead a man to give up an ideal that carried him through many years of difficult preparation certainly cannot be taken lightly.

*

Change my heart, O Lord, change my heart.

*   *   *

The Law is what love would do.

*   *   *

I should perhaps choose another time to write because I am tired at night. A day of sorrows and joys. Father Joe told me one of the novices will be leaving. It is painful. A letter from Dimitris was a joy, though I feel for him. He seems to be trying to make culture his religion. He is a lawyer now.

A mixed group at the cottage, each with a special need.

I am feeling pressure to get on with the Centering Prayer book, yet I don't really have the space to think and write well. It rates serious time and attention. Lord, help me get it together.

Still not sure if I should get into the practicum at the House of Affirmation.

*   *   *

When I sit down in the evening and try to recall the day's text I so often draw a blank—indicative of how little I have done with it during the day. "The fascination of trifles obscures the good." I am so often taken up in mind with housekeeping details and the like that I don't dwell deeply on the great true issues.

A fully, busy day with the candidates, but all are gone now. I hope to be free to write tomorrow.

*　　*　　*

A sad day in Ray's leaving. A quiet day. A beautiful day—clear and cold. A happy day—Ben and Damian were voted in for solemn vows.

A couple of resolutions: After Compline: if I have not gotten at least thirty minutes of personal *lectio*, that will be done first, then yoga, then other things, watching the time for retiring so I can get up rested. In the morning: after Vigils, meditation in church or the early Mass and thanksgiving, then reading, study, or meditation with tea, according to need—no fuzzing.

On the whole I feel good—receiving the grace to be more responsive and alive. The candidates are affirming and challenging.

*　　*　　*

Jesus died to make up for my sins—he took them on and satisfied for them. I am to love as he loved—that is his new command: "Love as I have loved you." So I am to take on the sins of others and satisfy for them. It shouldn't surprise me then or make me feel something unjust is happening when I have to bear the burden or brunt of others' sinfulness. It is as it should be, because Jesus has borne the brunt of my sins.

*　　*　　*

We had a bit of a shock today. We were gathered in the chapter room, voting on the solemn profession of Ben and Damian. Suddenly the door opened, and Father Henry stood there making the sign "dead." Who died? Names raced through my head. Then we realized he was telling us to "dead" (turn off) the microphone—everyone in the whole monastery could hear what was going on in the chapter. The signs do have their limitations!

Death always seems close to us, in our midst—we pass our brothers' graves constantly. Some of our seniors seem ripe for heaven. We all look to going to be with the Lord. Death is a joyful graduation, a commencement of the fuller life.

*　　　*　　　*

To be free and to love all properly requires being free to love them and ourselves in God, the creator.

*　　　*　　　*

Feast of the Conversion of Saint Paul

Saint Paul does not come across as an attractive or particularly likeable person. Perhaps we are a little jealous of his instant conversion, getting knocked off his high horse. It takes us ages to get down off our mount. He seems a bit arrogant. He doesn't hesitate to boast. Even in the midst of the turmoil of arrest he asserts, "I'm from Tarsus, no mean city." He is a Pharisee from the Pharisees. I think though it is his absolutely total commitment to Christ that tends particularly to rub us the wrong way. It scrapes right across our consciences. Such totality lays low our lukewarmness. And his life reminds us too poignantly that Christian life involves the Cross. Yet Paul is really a very humble man, and very human. "But for the grace of God. . . ." "I begged the Lord to take this sting of the flesh from me. . . ." I can easily identify with these sentiments. I know the sting of the flesh, and I beg, too, for deliverance. I don't hear directly words from the Lord, but I do believe his grace is sufficient for me.

Held in his love, I can believe that all will be well. More, I experience days of joy. How to reconcile this deep, constant, abiding joy and all the misery of our sinful condition? At base, I don't think we can or ought. It is. Even as our healing progresses—and it is a lifetime job to be completed only when the Master comes at the end—this joy abides. We love Christ, and we realize his glory, at least insofar as the creation is concerned, lies in being Savior—"The Son of Man came not for the just but for sinners." My sins, or, rather, their healing, augment his glory. Not that I should sin more so that he will have more glory! No. But being the poor, weak sinner that I am, I can count on him and be happy, knowing his happiness and glory in saving me.

Praise to Jesus, Lord and Savior!

* * *

Tremendous epistle today: The Father chastizes his beloved child. We can take all trials as the Father's chastizing.

*

I moved my office and cell to the cellarer's building today, to make more room for the new men coming. Looking back, I see it was exactly five years ago today that I moved up from the cellarer's. How curious that it should be exactly the same day! And where will I be five years from now? Still shuffling back and forth? Maybe that is a good definition of monastic life—shuffling back and forth, waiting to go to heaven.

* * *

Feast of the Presentation of Christ in the Temple

We are Jacob, the second sons. And we have a Mother who clothes us in the sweet-smelling garments of the First Born, covers our immature softness with his manliness, takes the poor fruit of our labor and transforms it into something delectable to our Father, and then enables us to receive the full blessing of the First Born. Happily, he is in no wise jealous of us, but wants this for us and gave us his Mother precisely so she could help us: "Behold your Mother!"

Mary, on this day present us to the Father in his temple of glory. And may all the just rejoice and proclaim what good things the Father does for us because of you, O holy Mother, sword-pierced Lady of tenderest love.

*

Saint Luke belongs to that joyous dancing tradition of the Hasidim. He is constantly bursting into song. Mary sings, Zachary sings, the angels sing, even old Simeon sings. From the time of Miriam at the banks of the Red Sea, there has always been a place for the ecstatic, for joy until folly among God's people. David in his loin cloth before the Ark will ever be despised by the more proper, so conscious of their dignity. But we will still waste our lives singing and dancing in our rituals before the Lord. We monks are the heirs to this tradition—we and all who know there is something more to life than meets the eye, and waste time, even much of our lives, celebrating it. My spirit rejoices in God my Savior, says the greatest of us, the little girl from the hill country, from the hick town, who is pregnant with Divine Life.

*   *   *

First Saturday—a very wonderful retreat in our hermitage. I received a great grace to finally give up all ambition to be somebody special and to accept whatever role the Lord gives me. At the moment it seems to be that of a monastic student, studying the Cistercian reality to try to live it fully and express it as best I can, and to further this study by others in different ways. I can see how this might lead in time to a more eremetical life. But at the moment I still have a great desire for spiritual paternity. I am grateful for the "sons" I now have and humbly hope God will let me serve them and let me serve others.

I also intend to keep a deep union with Tom. While in me he can live the monastic response he wanted, in him I can live the married vocation for God. The children of his flesh will be the children of my spirit. I know he will want this too. But I realize that in all this I might not be fully accepting the sterility of the desert, of the monastic vocation. Maybe God will take it all from me—then I will know.

I read in *Separation du monde* the four steps in Saint Anthony's vocation: asceticism, fighting with the devil, interior transformation, apostolic life. I seem to be mostly in the second—fighting against the capital sins ("out of her Christ cast seven devils"). I must still try to be more ascetical in fasting, etc. I hope that the transformation (purity of heart, *apatheia*, hesychasm, vision) is taking place and that I am also going out to others in loving service and bearing fruit. I hope I am not hurting others, giving them pseudo-fruit. I hope I am attaining true freedom to truly love in the Lord.

I tried to say the fifteen decades of the Rosary, meditating on each in between. I realize how I have neglected meditation on the Passion for a long time now, often so taken up with creative work that I find it hard to silence all to attend to the Lord in the depths of his mysteries.

I am very grateful for this day and for the hermitage. I offered Mass there, praying many prayers. I made many prostrations, as Saint Benedict would have us. I hope now to offer Mass again this evening with one of my boys for all the others and for him.

All thanks to the loving heart of Mary.

*   *   *

The Annual Retreat

Father is giving us quiet, reflective conferences on the word of God and the Rule. My own thoughts dwell on simply waiting on the Lord—patience, if nothing else; doing and accepting all as in him, for him, because he wants it. So simple, so little, but in practice often so hard—at least I fail so often.

*

The same is true when praying the Jesus Prayer. But I have found praying the psalter very fruitful. I had intended to pray the whole of it today, but succeeded in getting through only about thirty-two psalms.

*

Never seek God without the cross.
——Saint John of the Cross

*   *   *

We are into the retreat. Father Hugh is drawing on the apothegmata, those delightful stories so full of wisdom. First he stressed *conversatio* as being "on the move"—the counterbalance to stability. Keep going; use every second of life. We receive at best little more than a quarter million of them. Then he touched on the role of the spiritual father and our relations with him. He stressed the responsibility of each of us to father Christ in each other. The Cistercians, coming more immediately from the Gospels, would say, rather, mother the Christ in ourselves, each other, and the whole Church.

*

We had exposition yesterday. I sat all afternoon rather stupidly before the Lord. What else could I do? "I am like a dumb ox before you." My words are useless and unneeded. My heart is shallow and without fire. But I wanted to be there, before the Divine Medala, fascinated, centered by his special Presence. "Where can I go from his Presence?" "To whom shall we go? You have the words of eternal life." "Speak, Lord, your servant wants to hear." And he does speak to my heart. "I will lead him into the desert and there I will speak to his heart." It is desert. In ways, I am deserted. Yet in some mysterious deep way he seems to speak. And I don't want to go away—even though I can't say what he said. "The heart has its language of which the mind knows nothing." Speak, Lord, your servant wants to hear. Especially during these days of retreat, please, Lord, speak—speak to me and to each of my brothers—speak your words of eternal life. We do want to hear.

*

The Lord makes me realize more and more what a useless instrument I am. Unless his grace operates, nothing is accomplished. I only work harm. I puzzle over the problem of response to the brethren's needs and contemplation. I seem so taken up with my brethren and the things I am asked to do and see to be done for the community that I seem to find little time to rest quietly in the Lord. These needs drive me to prayer with tears, but it is not exactly contemplative. Should I try to forget others more? It seems unchristian. Yet how else rest quietly in the Lord—isn't this what a contemplative should do? Of course the Lord sees all the cares and concerns in our hearts. I don't have to tell him. Just be before him; he will see.

*

Rarely do I pray the Office well—so often distracted. I am trying to prepare it better and stay with the texts.

*   *   *

I find a font of tears which is wont to spring up speedily in lowly ground as in the valleys of a contrite soul.

——William of Saint Thierry

*   *   *

Last week was our annual retreat. I really missed it pretty completely. I was much too busy—and tired—and fell asleep at the conferences most of the time. Others really appreciated them. I guess I unconsciously felt I had had my retreat last fall, had too much to do, couldn't really bring my problems to Father and had this week's retreat planned.

Now I am sitting in a millionaire's home placed completely at my disposal for whatever time I want, probably until Thursday. I spent the morning driving here after teaching at

Spencer. I spent the afternoon, after a big meal served by Brother Hillary and Father Marianus, talking with the Prior, Father Raphael. He is a wise man, deeply committed to Carthusian contemplative values (at times they seem a bit triumphalistic, but in no offensive way), very kind and yet no nonsense. We talked of my vocational concern.

I see my life moving to a point where I can make a real option for contemplation. The question: Is this what God wants for me?

First of all—what does this mean? I take it to mean, first of all, really wanting, as the activity and happiness of my life, prayer-union with God, rather than activity-union. This pushes me a step farther back: wanting union with God as the happiness of my being, then I must practically choose this. Here is where the basic failure and trouble probably lie. At Vespers today we heard: *Scindite corda vestra et non vestimenta vestra!* Tear open your hearts and not your clothes. I think I have been projecting the responsibility of my failures on my life situation and thinking about changing it, when I should be going to my heart and seeking conversion there. Do I now make the decisive option for

- *First:* God.
- *Second:* Union with him as my happiness
- *Third:* Union with him through prayer
- *Fourth:* and therefore my response to everyone and everything in the light of this option.

It is important to live in the *now* and not to try here and now to plan the response of the future.

The Psalms of Vespers spoke to this: 129: watching and waiting on the Lord from the depths of my misery; 130: not reaching for things beyond me but resting on my mother's bosom (prayer is mother to me); 131: not for me, David-king-*basileos*, to build the house for the Lord, but my son, a spiritual son will do the things I don't do. But here, too, take care—the desire to have "spiritual sons" can vitiate.

Given this fundamental option—can I hope to live it at Spencer? I am presuming that this is what God wants for me—a radical choice of union with him in prayer and a lifestyle that responds to this. It will mean a constant choosing. Can it be done at Spencer? Obviously it can *in abstracto. In concreto*—will too many persons and things present themselves demanding too much time and attention even for the making of options, so that there will not be sufficient freedom and time for prayer, with the consequence that I should therefore seek a situation more conducive, freer for prayer? I think I would respond at this point that the option can be made concretely at Spencer. But will I find enough of the kind of support I need to faithfully make the option? This I do not know.

If I can't find it at Spencer, can I find it elsewhere? It seems Oxford offers it. Possibly also Obazine.

*　　　*　　　*

A bright warm sun is already high above the horizon. It feels good—very good after the days of cold and dampness.

It is a tender time for us. Father Bernard seems on the point of departure after eighty years and more of religious life. He was my confessor when I was a novice twenty odd years ago, already a venerable senior. Now he is more in heaven than on earth. He has been in a coma since last evening. I have spent some time with him in prayer. He has the body of a hearty old peasant and the soul will have a long struggle getting out. It was beautiful last night to see the young monks gathered around him.

As the old body struggles for breath, shrunken almost to a skeleton, incapable of movement, the fire of the spirit so hidden in the ashes—what is human life? Certainly not primarily a thing of the body but a spiritual force, a presence—that draws us to Father even in his diminished state. Father Bernard is a saint, a mystic of a high order. Yet even this chosen friend of the Lord must undergo corruption, the poor old body failing in every way, yet enchaining a spirit that longs to be free.

What is the proper attitude toward the body? It is actually an immensely beautiful thing, a precise, complex creation with extraordinary inner reserves for continuance and healing. Something very special in God's creation, to be reverenced and cherished. Yet so apt to be insubordinate, to seek its own satisfactions apart from its God-given role as subordinate partner to the spirit. Like a child without discretion it needs to be firmly disciplined with evident love.

*   *   *

Father Bernard breathed the last of earthly air last evening. Now he lies in the transcept, looking a bit jaunty with a little smile on his lips and his knee up in the air. Maybe it is because he had genuflected so often in his eighty-plus years of religious life, but the undertaker could not get his leg to straighten out. So there he lies, looking quite happy in his cowl, the hood pulled down to cover the wound in his forehead which he got when he fell out of his chair last week. The rosary, always in his hand, peeps out from the ample sleeves. The Holy Rood Guild made him a handsome stole, which hides the raised knee a bit. Two Brothers sit at his side, reading the Psalms. Everybody seems happy. Heaven and earth are a bit closer. A saint lies in our church. Outside even the pneumatic drill that cuts through the frozen earth in the cemetery seems to be singing. It is bright and sunny, the brightness that rises off freshly fallen snow. It is a grace-filled time for a home and a family when Jesus pays that special visit and takes a loved one to himself. One can sense the whole house sort of building up to the very special Mardi Gras we will have tomorrow when we lay our dear brother to rest, celebrating another great victory for the Risen Lord. Alleluia! The Paschal candle burns brightly. Christ has risen and Bernard has entered into that victory.

*   *   *

This day has had a special brilliance: sun on the snow, a cloudless sky. The wind of its own accord cleared the snow from the section of the cemetery where we were to lay Father Bernard to rest, leaving the other graves cowled in Cistercian white. The funeral was at 2:30. A few cousins came from Hartford, a number of Father's old confreres from the Sacred Heart Brothers, including a novitiate companion ninety-six years young; Father David of Gethsemani, Brother Daryl of

Mistassini, Brother David of Nova Nada, Brother Dominic from Wrentham; but mostly it was just the community

It was a magnificent way to celebrate the Mardi Gras. What greater celebration to set us on the way for Lent and the anticipation of Holy Easter?

The Paschal candle burned out at Father's grave, and we wait for a new fire seven weeks hence.

At 6:30 we met in chapter to share a bit of our recollections of Father Bernard. Encouraging was the fact that this monk of translucent faith and mystic vision, who conversed familiarly with the Persons of the Trinity and the holy Virgin and the saints, whose face at times shone with Taboric light, was a man with a real temper and stubbornness which lay hidden beneath a great sweetness and gentle kindness toward all until senility left it unguarded and betrayed the great virtue that had kept it so carefully in check through the decades. One wonders what that must have demanded of Father through his over eighty years of religious life. We usually witness only men's failures and do not see the struggle that lies hidden in their quiet successes or that sometimes precedes their showing failure. Failure can be the humiliation that crowns the long battle to make it something exquisitely beautiful to God as it hones a saint in a way that not even he can perceive and be tempted to vitiate by any proud self-satisfaction. How wondrous and hidden are your works, O Lord! I have full confidence that in the end, just as with Father Bernard, you will complete in each one of us the work you have begun, until we are reunited in your Kingdom, the monks of Spencer chanting forever your glory.

It seemed so appropriate that after we laid Father to rest and the Abbot had gently dropped the first shovel-full of dirt over his white cowl, we chanted the Magnificat: My soul magnifies the Lord and my spirit rejoices in God my Savior. For he that is mighty has done great things for me. Holy is his name!

May Bernard, our beloved Father, rest in peace and reign in glory!

THE LENTEN JOURNEY

Perhaps all monks are "little guys" like Zacchaeus. They want to see Jesus, but realize they can't succeed "in the crowd," so they go off and climb a tree (and get out on a limb!). Sometimes it takes a while to find the right tree—the one they can successfully climb.

As vocation father, I help a lot of fellows to size up our tree, to see if it is the right one for them. And then it takes time to climb a tree. Some are slower climbers than others. But if we keep at it—with the help of our God-given energies and that of our brothers—we will finally mount above the clamor of our passions and the obscuring attachments that hold us earthbound, and come to a point where we can see Jesus more and more clearly. And then, one day—as Saint Bernard and all the Fathers assure us—the Lord will take notice of us (though of course he was watching every move we made and cheering us on with his grace).

Yes, the Word will visit our house, and in that day we will find new freedom. We will be able to let go of the things of this world which we have acquired and become attached to—and even joyfully let go of them. We won't need our tree any longer. We will want to enter the inner sanctuary of our own selves and enjoy the intimate personal presence of our Lord.

It is at such a moment that some can feel drawn to leave the supportive structures of community life—as something no longer needed and which can impede the freedom to dwell within—and turn to the eremitic life. Others find that the established rhythms and fraternal care of community life offer the most freeing context. They would find all the involvement of setting up and maintaining their own establishment a greater hindrance to their freedom to be with the Lord than are the familiar structures of the communal life. Others, for a time, realize the call to a certain activity, to repay what they have taken or received and to dispense to those who are in need. This may be in the context of community services, or sharing something of the riches of the contemplative life with those in the crowd.

But all this must take second place. Primary is the response to the Lord, the hospitality that responds to his expressed desire to dwell in our house, in the inner chamber of our heart—certainly not to be left alone there, nor to be busily served with all the attention of the much-serving Martha. He wants some of the attention of Mary—Mary of Bethany, sitting at his feet, for we are disciples who still have much to learn; Mary of Nazareth, who pondered—weighed—his words, his actions—let them settle and rest in her heart, for us. For we, too, are to mother the Christ, in ourselves, in each other, in the whole Body, until he be fully formed. Like the bride who rests in his embrace and gives him the delight of letting him do whatever he wills, we want to be responsive to all of his attentions as he calls us forth to ever greater delight in his love.

You have made us for yourself, O Lord. . . .

* * *

Retreat, Thursday and Friday after Ash Wednesday

1. Keep my ideal, the meaning of my life, more clearly before me——to be fully one with Jesus.

2. To expand my horizons to his universal concern. To live with him in all that each day brings, for his intentions, his desires.

3. To gently, lovingly mother Christ in everyone I come into contact with
   - old as well as young
   - unattractive as well as attractive
   - trying, dull, or slow, as well as responsive and bright

4. To try during this Lent to take on a true attitude of self-mortification and self-sacrifice with and for Christ, not only in fasting, but in a whole life context.

Jesus, help me!

Mary, too.

*

Schedule:

2:30— 3:30	Prayer
3:30— 4:15	Vigils
4:15— 6:45	Prayer/*lectio*
6:45— 7:45	Lauds, Mass
7:45— 8:00	Prayer
8:00—12:30	Work, Terce, Sext
12:30— 1:00	Dinner
1:00— 2:00	Rest, light reading
2:00— 2:30	None, walk
2:30— 5:00	Work
5:00— 5:40	Prayer/*lectio*
5:40— 6:10	Vespers
6:10— 7:40	Oddements
7:40— 8:00	Compline
8:00— 9:00	Prayer
9:00—10:00	Reading

*

An action suffers if not preceded by consideration.

*

Spiritual labor is better expressed by the metaphor of
a sweating peasant.

——Saint Bernard

*   *   *

This morning I offered Mass in the cottage with the candidates. (In accord with early monastic custom, when Mass was
first becoming a daily practice for monks, we do not have a
community Mass in the church on Mondays.) For our chalice
we had a beautiful blue cup that came from Japan, the product
of a cottage industry. The family that made it was not Catholic,
nor even Christian, but Shinto. The cup was the type they used
for making libations to their ancestors, the source of their life.

We use it now to make an offering to our Creator, the Source of all life.

For the paten or communion plate we had a long, slender, metal fish made by American Indians. They, too, are not Christians. For them, the fish is a symbol of the Spirit moving freely amidst the waters of life. They capture him and eat him, to be nourished by him and to receive his spirit and life. For us Christians, from our earliest times the fish has been a symbol of Christ, who is our Divine Food in this holy meal and gives us his Spirit and Life. The Indians cast this fish in the sand and polished it to a gleaming sheen; they mixed eight or ten different metals to attain a certain richness and durability. It will be in the coming together in the one Christ of the many cultures that we will be able to come to that fullness of beauty and strength that can undergird our crumbling world society and make it a thing of immense beauty.

*   *   *

It is proving to be a very quiet and peaceful Lent. Lots of quiet space for prayer. Not particularly dark prayer. Nor lightsome prayer. Prayer that just *is*, touching the "Is" of God—entering into the great "I" who has always been and will always be, in whom I have always been and always will be. It seems to matter little that this particular expression of the loving beneficent thought of God began to unfold at a particular moment in time. It is in his "I" that I really am.

I feel as if my life were over. I have done enough, accomplished enough, done enough of this and that. Now it is sufficient just to be. Yet, in another sense, more truly, my life is just beginning. It is always just beginning. Each day, many times a day, at each moment, I come to a new level of being, a new quality of being, and it is all new. "Behold, I make all things new."

Praise to you, Lord Jesus Christ, King of eternal glory.

*

Jesus was very present during confession on Sunday. It was one of his special visits. It is the beginning of what I believe and hope will be a very special Lent.

*   *   *

Feast of the Annunciation

The Incarnation was prepared for both by our evolutionary development and by our sins. That is the wonder of our God, so good and so powerful. Even our sin can be fully drawn into his plan of glory.

*   *   *

Quidquid recipitur per modum recipientis recipitur—the one Thomist principle that has remained with me—at least in Latin—from my years of studying scholastic theology. *Quidquid recipitur*—whatever is received is received according to the mode of the receiver.

God's light shines upon every man, woman, and child on the earth. Each receives it according to who he or she is. "The fascination of trifles obscures the good." For how many of us, how much of the time is the Sun of Justice clouded over, smogged out by trifles, by the pollution we allow our curiosity and our passions to belch forth in our minds and in our hearts! We need an inner ecology that begins with screening imports—our reading, our listening, our wandering. The value of the cell and of silence appear here. But we need even more to quiet the inner movie theater, let the screens go blank. Sit in the darkness and let the pure light of God flood in unimpeded. His white light contains all the spectrum—in him we can find all the color of life in fullness, perfectly integrated in perfect harmony. We give up nothing. . . . We find all and in fullness.

*

Go not outside, return into yourself; the Truth dwells in the inner man.

——Saint Augustine

*

In the inner man dwells God, the Truth, who cannot
be reached by those who seek him in externals—God,
whose nature it is to be always and only within and in
the most inward place.

————Meister Eckhart

*

In order to arrive at having pleasure in everything,
desire to have pleasure in nothing.
In order to arrive at knowing everything,
desire to know nothing.
In order to arrive at possessing everything,
desire to possess nothing.
In order to arrive at being everything,
desire to be nothing.

————Saint John of the Cross

*

As I let go of seeking gratification on the level of the
senses and of the satisfactions of the world: success, recogni-
tion, power of sorts, there awakens more lustily a desire for
satisfaction on the level of thought and ideas. This too must be
left behind. But even when the whole of the "I," the ego, the
superficial levels of personality, are left behind, it is not yet
enough. It is only when the deepest "I" loses itself by being
wholly present to the "I am" and, as it were, is absorbed in
pure consciousness in him that the transformation of consciousness, the dying to self is complete and the risen life in
Christ finally is. We can experience this, it seems, only tran-
siently in this life. When we choose to abide there constantly,
we choose to pass into a new life, leaving behind all the
divided attention of this pilgrimage. But we can have those
transient moments—however long they might actually be by
chronos—and they are among the most precious of our jour-
neying, a God-given viaticum that fills us with hope and joy.

*

We must plunge ourselves into the nothingness from which creation comes, there to discover the all of God and our oneness with him. Man can be recreated only in the place where he was created. Baptism plunges us into this death so that we can rise to the new life. All our ascesis is but an appropriation of what is already ours by Baptism. Any way that stops short of this is ultimately un-Christian.

*

Thought, however lofty, always belongs to the level of signs and therefore of its nature demands to be transcended in the direct vision of the Reality signified.

*

Christ is the self-awareness of the Father. In coming to truly know ourselves, images of God, we come to know the Image. Through true self-awareness we come to know God. *Noverim me ut noverim te.* When the Church, in its ministers, ministers to our needs to move toward this inner awakening to ourselves, it most truly responds to our needs and to its mission to lead us through the incarnate reality to the knowledge and experience of the Divine. "We once knew Christ in the flesh, but we know him so no longer." We are to pass beyond the flesh to the Divine in and through the Spirit.

*

To be seized inwardly by the devouring Presence, to undergo the experience that will utterly transform and produce a true *metanoia*, a total conversion, this is fundamental to lived Christianity.

*

God will not deign to be loved along with anything that is not loved for his sake.

*   *   *

Reason unaided by love can lead us only to pride.

*   *   *

I enjoy the poetry of the Psalms:

> I lie on my bed and moan
>   Like some lonely bird on the roof. . . .

This verse from Psalm 101 sometimes resonates deeply with my feelings. The "moan" catches exactly how I feel. But then I picture myself perched on the pinnacle of the church roof, perhaps my bed teetering precariously beneath me, or just crouched like an ungainly oversized bird, trying to keep my footing on the slippery green tile, leaning against a lightning rod, bemoaning my miserable life. . . . This ludicrous image is enough to shake me rapidly loose from my undue self-pity. I am not sure that this is exactly what the Psalmist had in mind, but it helps.

I do have my aches and pains, my frustrations and miseries. But taken in perspective they hardly justify a lot of moaning and groaning. Looking at them in the light of what so many of my brothers and sisters in so many parts of the world, and even in the light of what some of my brothers here at Spencer, have to bear, mine are very small indeed. And when they are seen and experienced in the context of who I really am and what is actually going on in my life . . . a sinning sinner, my just deserts call for much worse. As redeemed, a son baptized into intimate oneness with the very Son, my blessings and glory far outshadow my pains and miseries.

As one privileged to be a co-redeemer with my Master, my heartaches and pains are precious. With his they become almost infinite in their power to win healing and redemption for myself and all who are dear to me and all the human family. If "I lie on my bed and moan," it is more from joyful, painful, wonder-filled longing for the fullness of what I already perceive in the first shadows of dawn.

*   *   *

We all have our favorite Scripture texts. They are the ones where at one time or another the Lord spoke to us in that special way that is proper to him alone. And we return to them again and again, hoping he will speak once more, or at least that some echo of that special experience will be heard again . . . that that fire will glow again in our heart.

It doesn't usually happen that way. Our God is a God of surprises. He likes to come upon us when and where we least expect—on the garden path, after we have searched long for him at the tomb. We don't want to succumb to the temptation of a certain "magic": Yesterday when I prayed in the garden near the statue of Saint Anne at sunrise, kneeling on my heels, saying the Jesus Prayer, he came—one of those wonderful "visits of the Lord," as Saint Bernard calls them—so this morning I am there again at the same time, again on my heels, with the Prayer going. But instead of being deeply in the Prayer, ready for the visit, I am all caught up in seeking the visit, seeking the experience for myself—indeed, seeking myself, my pleasure, my satisfaction.

It doesn't work that way. I can vouch for this from experience. But still when the Lord does really speak to us through a special Scripture text, I think it is good to keep returning to that text. He may not speak so powerfully again, but I think his initial use of the passage is an invitation from him to return to it again and again, to draw from its limitless sources. And so I go again and again to favorite texts like John 14–17, 1 Corinthians 2, Revelation 3, Philippians 2 and let them reecho the graces of before and bring today's daily bread. "Speak, Lord, your servant wants to hear." He speaks to me where I am today and gives me today's food for the journey.

*

For Christian faith, there is no doubt that the knowledge of the Gospel revelation and the impact of Jesus'

own experience marks a critical point in the development of what men call the experience of God.
——Abhishiktananda

*   *   *

We are reading in the refectory an essay by one of our modern liberal Catholics. For him Christ seems to be mainly a theological question; God is our own personal concoction as an explanation for the ultimates in our lives. One wonders if this man ever really prayed, ever experienced the loving, caring presence of his heavenly Father. How different life is when we can say with Saint Paul: "I know in whom I have believed." We are not worthy, but he himself made the decision: "I will no longer call you servants, but friends." How good it is to be a friend of God; painful at times in the face of my infidelities, but a pain I will gladly suffer rather than lose anything of that friendship.

*   *   *

Arise, God, dispense justice throughout the world, since no nation is excluded from your ownership.
——Psalm 82:8

All is the Lord's: China, India, Tibet, as much as Italy, Israel, and the United States. People and individuals might recognize and respond to this lordship in widely varying ways and degrees. Yet it stands. All that is good, beautiful, and true among any peoples and cultures is the Lord's and of the Lord. To recognize this and rejoice in it is to be truly catholic. All things are ours and we are Christ's and Christ is God's. There is nothing that is alien to us except sin, and that is nothing, a lack of due goodness.

Strangely, we are sometimes more willing to let sin invade our lives than to accept some of the beauty and truth of other cultures and religious expressions. In our hearts we can dance with the Hare Krishna, whirl with the Sufi, tumble with King David before the Ark, knowing that the God they all seek to exalt is enthroned within us. Our love embraces the liturgy of the whole creation and everyone therein and lifts it up to our God enthroned. There is nothing in the world of goodness, truth, and beauty that is not the Lord's and to be returned to him with love.

Mother Teresa of India sees this in the dying "rubbish" she gathers from the streets. (How merciful a God he is, that he can even forgive us for making our fellow-humans "rubbish"! How far can we push the mercy of God? And it is we in the affluent, wasteful, consuming, militarized nations who are most responsible for creating this human "rubbish." Lord, have mercy.) Teilhard de Chardin saw it in the geological strata and the story of the earth. Abhishiktananda perceived it in the advaitic experience of Hindu mystics. And Sister Jose Hoday points to it in the rich life-ritual of the Papagos.

Whether our minds and even our feet range far and our perceptions are deep or our horizons rarely lift above the details of daily living to the starry vaults above, all is of the Lord and invites us to a catholic liturgy as a priestly people, bringing all to the glory of God in Christ. "Whether you eat or drink or whatsoever else you do, do all for the glory of God."

*

If we are unable to change the war-making climate, we can at least strive not to be changed by it, but remain in Jesus, peacemakers, healers, reconcilers.

*   *   *

A guard over your lips is always useful, but not one that excludes gracious affability.

*

The best kind of vision occurs when you are self-sufficient and need nothing in order to know everything you wish to know. Moreover, to be assisted from without is to become dependent, and this is to be less than perfect and less than free.

——Saint Bernard

*

Christ is my master. I am challenged by the example of some of the young, and not so young, who come along these days. They have taken this swami or that roshi as their master. They are very proud of him and readily speak of him to others and try to win others to him. Yet so often we seem hesitant to speak proudly of Christ, our Master, and to try to lead others to accept him as their master. The way these men talk and live— organizing their life's activities according to the instruction they have received—gives strong witness to their conviction that their master has the goods.

Does the way I speak and live give strong witness to my conviction about Christ, my Master? More deeply, do I really respond to Christ as master? Do I think and live as his disciple? Is my life centered on this: following Christ, being his follower, following his way as the way? Beyond the masters these men follow, Christ is so much more; so much more in himself—very God, infallible, all-loving, all-present—and so much more to me: friend, intimate, lover. But that is harder to talk about. "My secret is mine, my secret is mine."

*

The whine of the little space heater fills the silence and yet does not intrude. All is silence. The abbey is a good place— there is so much silence, place, space. I need that. Wednesday, Roger asked why I was not going to lunch with the others. I could and probably should have. But I was enjoying the space and quiet of that hour between all the talking, listening, and empathy.

I have grown used to having a lot of space as my own. More than I realized. I begin to feel busy and crowded if I do not get several hours of quietness in the day. What I claim as minimal I guess most would consider a luxury. Married life, so constantly with a spouse and family, would be hard to take, so crowded, so unfree, so demanding. I sense God is ever present, but he is not in some sense demanding. Though he asks for all—he gives a lot of space. When I am alone at his level it is all so good.

*

Simplicity is nothing else than an act of pure and simple charity, having one only aim and end, which is to acquire the love of God, and our soul is simple when in all that we do or desire we have no other aim.
——Saint Francis de Sales

*   *   *

The biggest enemy to my freedom is "me"—my habits and my stupidity.

*

"Seek and you shall find."

The Lord, who made us, respects us and respects the way he made us. He respects our psychological make-up. It is the one who is really seeking who has the openness to see and hear and find. When we hear his word in the Liturgy or in our personal reading, it is only if we are really seeking as his servants to hear him speak to us that we will really hear the word and find the enlightenment we seek. He respects the freedom he has given us and he will not push his way in and overpower us with his light. It is the one who freely decides for him, wants him and therefore seeks him, who will find him and his *truth* and *light*.

*   *   *

Much of the time I just sit before the Lord. And that is about it. It is love that puts me there and love that keeps me there. I give myself to him. What more is there to do? What more is there to give? That is all I have. It is existential prayer. I belong to Mary. So she is in it too. It is as simple as that.

*   *   *

Palm Sunday

Last week was almost an impossible week: Monday—monastic vocation directors of New England; Wednesday—the young priests of Bridgeport diocese; Thursday—meetings and an evening penitential service; Friday—the young priests of Boston archdiocese—and a cottage full of candidates. But through it all the Lord was very present, even though a cold kept me from Vigils and the early prayer. Now into the deep reality of Holy Week. Today was a beautiful start.

*   *   *

It seems to have been a long day—the trip to the House of Affirmation, correspondence, candidates, etc. But at last it is over and quiet. Roger asked why I keep so busy (and then gave his own answer, as we so often do when we question others). One reason is I enjoy the things I do. I have a lot of energy. I see them as being helpful to others. I don't see them as interfering with what I want most in life. Yet I am now seeing that I have not attended enough to some of my needs and desires in attending to others, and have not made a conscious choice to do this, thus engendering a certain amount of frustration. Now that I see what has been going on I feel better, more in control, and I will perhaps make some changes.

Sometimes I find myself wanting to relate more deeply with others, and yet at the same time wanting to keep my independence—an ambiguity. How do I resolve it? I need the community in some ways—in other ways I do not. I need it because I choose to make it my community, and my brothers accept me and I need community somewhere. On the other hand I do not need it, because if for some reason it cannot be my community I can find another. Actually the community has done very well by me. But I have held back in some ways in responding to the community and they do react to this. I need to give myself more, especially to some, and also to be realistic in my expectations of the community. With such realizations come peace and a deeper acceptance.

It will be a good Easter.

*

Holy Thursday

Our God is a spacious God, and we are called to be as he is. We need to give others space—good space, supportive space, filled with affirmation and caring love. So that, if they chance to fall—even the just man falls seven times a day—they will be cushioned with acceptance and can easily arise and go on. God never withdraws his affirming creative love, no matter how often we fall. And he is always ready to forgive and help us. He gives us good space. So ought we to give good space to one another.

* * *

Good Friday

God is now. We experience creation in a linear fashion, events succeeding events. God sees all creation in a single act, pinnacling in that moment when the fullness of divine love was expressed in a created heart in a most dramatic sign—at the moment when God-become-man willingly let his human substance be sundered by death as an expression of his love. We can make that most significant moment of creation present at any moment by our faith. It is more forcefully and effectively present when the Christian community places the sacramental sign of it according to the charge of the Lord. It is most effectively present when the whole of the Christian Church relives in sacramental mystery the ultimate moments of the Lord in the Great Week.

There is a special presence of this crowning act of created reality when a follower of the Master gives witness to him and his act by the ultimate following, willingly embracing the opportunity to express love in a similar act—the gift, the privilege of holy martyrdom—a grace that throws its special light on our Holy Week experience this year as we live again in an age of martyrs. When Pope John XXIII called for a new Pentecost, we did not advert to the fact that Pentecost was soon followed by an ever-expanding call to martyrdom. And then, monasticism . . .

Holy Saturday

Day of emptiness! Day of hope!

So empty—no Liturgy, no Sacrament, no lamps in the house of the Lord, only darkness, stillness, emptiness—and waiting.

So full of hope—for us who know, we wait on tiptoe. A day with Mary. Every Saturday is hers because on this Saturday the whole of the hope of the Church was summed up in her. We wait with Mary, trying to enter into her sentiments. How deep the pain, the sense of loss—the sword, indeed, has pierced and ripped open this Mother's heart. We enter in. Dare we? Is not this sanctuary too holy for us? Will we not violate it? Yet where better can we learn? She pondered—weighed—all these things in her heart.

Here hope waits for its greatest victory, its greatest fulfillment.

With Mary, in Mary we wait
   —till the great new Paschal candle, lit by the new
    fire, leads us down the cloisters, into the
    Church, into the holy Paschal season, into the
    ceaseless Alleluias——for he will *rise* again
                   —in us!
           Alleluia! (anticipated)

*

It is gray and bleak outside, cold and chill, befitting the sadness and emptiness of this day. A beautiful sunrise would have been out of place, though I hope we will be blessed with such tomorrow.

*

The week has been one of deep quiet. I have been present to the reality, less to the Liturgy. I seem to be more free. This has in some ways been the busiest Holy Week I have ever had. Not busy in a busy sort of way but in another sense. Since high school days I have dropped everything for this week and lived it alone, often very busy in a busy way with Liturgy, choir, sacristy, etc. This year I am more out of all these things, more in other things—the meeting on Wednesday at the House of Affirmation, candidates, keeping the office going, etc. But all was quietly, realistically blending into the unfolding reality of Christ's living and dying this week. I feel good about it. Very close to Jesus. Our friendship and sharing are deeper than ever.

Dana came out last night—brought me an Easter lily. I love him very much. I hope things will work out for him. We will drive to Michigan together for the Cistercian conference. I am delighted with the lily, which is just opening. Flowers, plants, growing things delight me. I would have loved to be a father, to watch over the growth of my own child. Sharing with Mike his wonder over Travis was great. And yesterday came Ken's note—Harmony Joy was born at home on the 27th. What a beautiful experience it was for him and Bobbie! Harmony will be baptized tomorrow.

I do feel a great joy already. But I want to be with Mary today and experience something of the emptiness and longing so that there will be more space to be filled in the morning.

Come, Risen Lord, rise in our lives!

NIGHT OF FIRE

&

DAYS OF LIGHT

Easter

Christ is risen!
He is truly risen!

A good tiredness after a very full day. The richness of the
Vigil was quietly, deeply beautiful. A wonderful breakfast *en
famille* which lasted well over an hour. Lauds at 7:30; then
candidates. Some hard ones: Tom is to stay with his own
group—that went fairly well; Kerry is to get psychiatric help—
that was tough. He feels so hurt and rejected. He has been
turned out by his own family and has no place to go, and he
badly needs help. He has repeatedly been refused, or accepted
and then sent away by religious institutions. He is really psychotic. The crosses some have to bear! Lord, do take care of
Kerry! There doesn't seem to be much I can do, but to refer
him and pray. He can only sense this as another rejection.
Brian showed up unexpectedly—back from his Hawaiian out-
ing, looking well, gung-ho to enter. Dana is developing well.
We are looking forward to our trip.

*

The community has grown much in its love. Everyone
seems to sense this. We have much cause for joy and gratitude,
and that is what I feel. The day has been perhaps a bit too
full—not enough time just to sit with the Lord, though I did
get in a meditation before Vespers and after, and an hour by
the fire after supper.

Amen. Thank you, Jesus, my Risen Lord.

*

I am struck by our Lord's great delicacy and compassion,
his concern for others, as he appears on Easter night to the
Apostles. He himself was undergoing a tremendous experi-

71

ence—life in a resurrected body, with all the qualities of such a body. How he wanted to share this overflowing joy with his friends, the wonder of it! (I find it hard to attribute to him the all-too-human desire we might have had to go back to the High Priest and Pilate and Herod and scare them out of their wits.) Yet, as he came into the midst of the Apostles, his concern was for them. He had tried to prepare them with prophecies and the resurrection of Lazarus. Still they were slow in comprehension—and we are slow. So he tried to help them: See, feel—flesh and bones. He wanted them to touch, to feel him. He asked for food and ate for them, with them. He took them step by step till his joy in his resurrection was theirs also. How patient even now he is with our slowness to believe!

We need his help to believe that all he has taught us is true. What we find most difficult to believe is not the truth about him, but the truth about ourselves, our goodness, beauty, worth—that we really are the beloved children of God, that all our sins and misery, our great stupidity, do not make all that much difference to him.

*   *   *

Easter Monday

A full holiday—the Orthodox speak of it as the coming back of the feast. But it was not much of a holiday for me. I feel a bit depressed. I think it is mainly from working with Kerry. It seems to be all give and no response with a psychotic person. He was supposed have left early today but hung on and is still here. I don't think we can do any more for him, and he weighs on the whole atmosphere.

Scott is only fifteen. He has been brushed off by most of the vocation people he has approached, so he was warmed in receiving a real response here. He is an exceptional person but it will be a long haul before he will be able to enter the monastery. Bob is at the other end—thirty-five, but he probably needs as much in his own way.

And where am I?

The quiet is here. With Christ—all; without him—what?

Darkness, loneliness, fear. He is risen. Light. Hope.

*   *   *

Food is so much a part of our feast. This is good in a way. But one longs for a deeper communion.

The night is quiet. It is good to settle down to reading in the quiet cell. The desire to be with and yet the weariness of being with. The choices are mine. I make them. But with yet a desire for the other. The other—can I live without it? But can I live with both? I need to.

Peace. Quiet. Rest in the quiet. Love.

*   *   *

The little sun we enjoyed this morning is gone. More gray skies, cold, chill, and damp.

The oil burner is working hard; the radiators are singing their own perky tune. It would be good to have a fire. We will this evening.

I feel kind of down. Father Bill took Kerry off to the bus. I was really sorry for him and felt so helpless. Then I had a note from Ed, another poor lad, victim of a pathetic home situation, also mentally afflicted. Father Ambrose has been good to him. But where is he to find real healing? I don't know. Ultimately we must find all in the Risen Lord. But for now, a scared, lonely life, filled with lots of pain and a sort of hoping against hope that we will take him in. I wish there were a l'Arche in New England. How great is the need! I should write Phil and get a line on the ones in Canada.

Meeting men like Kerry and Ed and even Brian puts me in touch with my own helplessness. Really it is the Lord who effects all, but sometimes he doesn't want to work through me and I have to accept it. The mystery of sin and the effects of sin—so many and so varied!

There is still a big stack of mail on my desk. I let it pile up during Holy Week and now I'm feeling a bit of pressure to get through it, and to write the letters I need to write to line up the May trip which is really only a few days away.

There is a quietness and a restlessness. I am too quick. I catch myself in little ways: jumping in ahead on the singing, jamming keys on the typewriter . . .

*　　　*　　　*

The sun has just broken above a banding of horizon clouds into a completely open sky. It will be a beautiful day, and a busy one.

Yesterday had its special joys. Watching Debra give birth to three beautiful little ewes. They are beautiful. But I sure felt for Deb in the push. Then the meeting with Ed, finalizing plans for his return on June 4th. And then Jim's coming. I love the beautiful full human quality of this young priest. So fully human, gently loving, completely giving. But like so few others, knowing that an important part of his giving is the hours of prayer, reading, silence, and solitude, which are an important part of his life. He is very happy in his new assignment as spiritual director of the seminary, and getting more and more into the whole ministry to priests and college students, fostering vocations, growth in leadership in the Church.

We talked about my doing a book on priestly spirituality. He felt priests need to learn to live spacious lives to give them time for themselves and others without rush. I recalled the candidate who told me last week that he had been in touch with seven vocation directors, but I was the first one who ever really talked with him. I was a bit—if shocked is too strong a word—pained at my first meeting with vocation directors, hearing some of their attitudes toward inquirers. I find each man who comes an exciting, beautiful revelation of God and feel it a privilege to be the recipient of his sharing of his life and God's working in it.

*

The warmth of the sun shining through the window on my cheek feels good. The birds are singing, a crow cawing. The field of lilies around the Paschal candle is ahead of the outside, but in a more subtle way all trumpet the resurrection in the awakening of new spring life. I can hear the silence and it is full. I pause and listen to it, and it is more beautiful than music.

*

I am concerned about Brian, so good, pure, simple, but perhaps too free for us. Would our discipline help him or could it be caging a wild rabbit, meant to run about the forest, exploring the wonders of God in creation?

*   *   *

A bright sun floods through my window. But the oil burner is going, for it is still quite cold outside. Apart from its purr and the morning symphony of our feathered friends, all is quiet. The force and power of the sun is almost too great for me to say "peaceful." The great globe of fire seems too potentially energetic to convey a sense of peace. Perhaps, too, it is too evocative of what could become our globe if the nuclear holocaust does erupt—a globe of fire, consuming all till it wholly consumes itself, sending out a minuscule spurt of power and light into the vast galaxy and then becoming only a memory in the mind of God—an experiment that failed, save for a few—Jesus weeping over the global Jerusalem: "I would have . . . but you would not."

How God respects our freedom! It is frightening, but it is our glory. The dignity that summons us to hold our heads high—above the rest of creation; to humble ourselves before our God, and yet to respond to the most sublime, challenging, life-giving, exciting, and wonderful words that have ever been formed by human lips—the very lips of God—lips that kissed even as they said: "I no longer call you servants, but friends."

I hear those words spoken now in my inner being, or, rather, just the one word: *Friend*—and my whole inner being ripples with excitement. Trembles is not the word, though maybe it should be the reality, but neither is it a ripple. It is a deep, total responsiveness that wants to erupt into a total all-inclusive existential embrace. God is here, more in the fabric

of my being than I am myself, and he says: Friend! And the
embrace is total . . .

*   *   *

Easter Saturday

Ben prostrated himself at the foot of the Paschal candle.
And there, protruding from among the lilies, was a microphone to amplify his plea for "the mercy of God and the
Order." I am sure the Lord did not need help in hearing, but
maybe the Order did, grown ever more institutional with age.
Technology insinuates itself into the most ancient of rites: a
young man seeking the monastic cowl and the care of a spiritual father. Some sixty fathers walked up to embrace Ben and
assure him of love and care and an "Amen" to his plea for
divine mercy. Now Ben struggles with his new long sleeves
and begins to realize what he has promised and gotten himself
into—a beginning that will never be completed, for he and
God have been mystically bonded forever.

The family crowded into the church for the profession,
and, later, into the cloisters—Mom and Grandma getting their
first glimpse of the "inner sanctum." It makes so much sense.
One wonders why they had to wait six years to see the inside of
their son's home. The enclosure is important, to be sure. Everyone needs his or her sanctuary, a place of privacy with the
family. The monk needs his place apart to be free to his God.
But if that is not violated by letting Dad in, why must Mom be
kept out? It has never made much sense to me. Why there can
be tours at stated times and special times for men and not for
women is hard to understand. Even historically it does not
hold much water. And the results are curious. While women
are all but eternally excluded, often men are too freely ad-
mitted to the detriment of the sacred space, the silence and
solitude that the monk has come apart to seek.

If we have a balanced and deep love of our monastic
values we should be able to admit men and women with equal
discretion and prudence. If I have become so hypersensitive
that seeing a woman walk down the cloister is a problem for
me, then I should get out and work at restoring a sense of

proportion and balance. Women, of course, and men should respect the holiness and quality of the enclosure and speak and act and dress accordingly. That goes without saying.

We had a delightful reception in the library with lots of kielbasa, cheese and punch. I think half the Polish people of New England were on hand to celebrate the consecration of a Gargulinski. But it was undoubtedly the monks who enjoyed the Polish sausage more than did the Polish visitors. On such occasions it becomes quite evident that Christian monks do not abstain from meat because of convictions about its effect on their systems (maybe they have something to learn here from their Eastern brothers) but out of a sense of poverty and self-denial. They love the stuff—a gift from God, like all good food—and enjoy it to the full when they can get it. Beer and wine, too. At least most of them. We all thoroughly enjoyed the solemn profession of this son of Poland.

*   *   *

Working with grace, which is the operative presence of God within us, we see our options and make a choice by which we experience our freedom and with God create who we are going to be. To make a commitment is to establish ourselves in freedom, and to make a perpetual commitment is to establish ourselves in eternal freedom—God's freedom, the creative gift of self in love.

*

A monk accepts with gratitude and a certain surprise the joys that come to him; the trials he accepts as what he bargained for.

——Hubert Van Zeller

*

Negative reasons cannot adequately account for the monastic journey into solitude. Monastic renunciation is the answer to a positive call from God, inexplicable, not subject to scientific demonstration, yet able to be

verified by faith and the spiritual wisdom of the
Church.

——Thomas Merton

*

Like Charlie Brown's baseball team, the monastic community is a team that always loses: each monk must die to his false
self—his ego self—and the community as such accomplishes
nothing this world can applaud. If they do applaud our by-
products, we would be most foolish to accept this as applause
for who we truly are and what we essentially do. Such applause
only obscures the more valuable contribution we could make
to their lives by being a challenging stumbling block of irrele-
vance, a sign that points to nothing in this world, a challenge to
look beyond. May our success in our manual labor, done to
fulfill man's primal penance and secure our livelihood, not
undermine our true meaning either to ourselves or to others or
to God.

*   *   *

The monk remains a disciple, a pupil, his whole life long.
He doesn't graduate when he gets out of the novitiate or when
he makes solemn vows. And he'd better not think he has! For
the classes go on: the Liturgy, chapter talks, the refectory
reading, the whole routine of monastic life. If he considers
himself a graduate he will be at odds with all this. Not only will
he lose an openness to constant growth but he will be fighting
his environment: the School of the Lord's Service, the School
of Love. He will be unhappy because he will be trying to be
one thing—whatever he conceives the life of a graduate to
be—while everything around him and the whole structure of
life will constantly be confronting him with other expectations.
He is apt then to graduate from the monastic life—if such
leaving can be called a graduation—or to withdraw more and
more from the community and become a marginal person, not
unlike a bachelor outside the monastery who tries to shape his
own little world to his own comfort and satisfaction.

This is not so easy to do in the monastery because one is

constantly bumping into the brethren and the regulations of
the community. The only graduate the monastic community
recognizes is the hermit who, as Saint Benedict says, after long
years of training within the community, goes out to single-
handed combat with the blessing of the community and the
abbot or, even rarer, one who is called by the Church to
employ the fruits of his contemplative life to serve God and his
people in apostolic mission. There is only one Cistercian bishop
in the world today (perhaps three or four in the course of the
past century) and a few dozen hermits.

*   *   *

Those who put aside travel for the sake of perfection
go anywhere, instantly.
                    ——Elder to Jonathan Livingston Seagull

The monks' whole life is a liturgy, a hymn of love
endlessly sung in imitation of the angels.
                    ——A Monk of Pierre-qui-vire

*

If you cannot sing like the nightingale and the lark,
then sing like the crows and frogs, who sing as God
meant them to.
                    ——Thomas à Kempis

Low Sunday

There is a bright cheery bird chirping lustily outside my
window. The sun is well up, and it promises to be a pleasant
Sunday.

It will have its pain, as I have to talk to two candidates this
morning: the one an alcoholic in his late thirties, who has some
hopes; the other a thirty-year-old gay with a strong negative
self-image, yet who thinks he is all set to enter. It won't be easy
to let them down and reorient them without pain. Lord, help!

Yesterday was special in so many ways ... Ben's profession, the abbot's talk on the garden (it's about time something

was done about redeveloping it), the arrival of a small beef herd. Some beautiful candidates.

*

My window box is a delight. The amaryllis is sending out new leaves that curl—I never saw anything like it. The apparently dead vine cuttings are popping with fuzzy little leaves. The English ivy is reaching out anew. Everything is springing into renewed life. Is that why we call it spring?

Praise God for all the gifts of life!

*   *   *

This is going to be some day!

I have a cold, so I slept late and am off to a late start with all the miseries of a common cold.

I am in the midst of a Centering Prayer workshop with a group of vocation directors.

Shantidas is coming for a colloquium at one. I am to have supper with him at five.

The Lady Abbess of Stanbrook is coming at three for tea.

The vocation directors of the diocese are coming at seven for a meeting.

Mother Mary Clare is coming for an article which I promised by May 1st, but which is not yet done.

I wonder how I get into all these things. I suppose I could have declined meeting and eating with Shantidas and left it to others. And I could have told the Abbess I was too busy to see her, though she flies back to England tomorrow and she was very gracious to me when I was there. The vocation ministry is my work now. And the article is for the sixteenth centenary of Saint Basil's death, so I couldn't refuse that. And so—Lord, help! If I move quietly with each as it comes, all goes well in peace. Thank you, God.

*   *   *

We are beginning a Zen Retreat with Joshua Sasaki Roshi. I began the sitting, wondering why I was doing it. We have

gotten a lot out of TM, and Zen seems unnecessarily demanding and rigorous. But after my interview with Roshi I began to
feel it was worthwhile just for the sake of contact with him.
With his koan he is aiming at getting me to experience the
aloneness of God—all, here and now. The experience is making me realize how spiritually lazy I have been and, resultant-
ly, how much I have been living on the surface. Reverend
Father spoke this morning on anger, and that seems to be
something I could use more to get after myself for wasting so
much of life's energies.

*

One meditates in order to be in control of what goes
on within one instead of being controlled by it.
                              ——Thomas Merton

The human condition is immense poverty in tremendous potential.
                              ——Thomas Keating

*

As our world grows rapidly smaller, and our potential to
destroy in many varied ways grows greater, the need for unity
among the members of the human family, and especially
among the Christian community which is to be the leaven,
grows proportionately. It is not surprising then that the Lord
gives to more and more Christians of the West a more open
heart and a deeper understanding of the values and beauties of
other traditions, both Christian and non-Christian. Such a gift
is not given so that the person can abandon his own tradition.
That would not promote the needed unity; rather it would
promote more ill will, suspicion, and defensiveness.
    The one who receives such a gift receives a great gift; it
will greatly enrich his life. But as our Master said, to whom
more is given, more is expected. The burden is not always
light. The one to whom the Lord gives this insight and openness perceives more the lacks in his own limited tradition—all
traditions are limited and have their lacks, some more than

others—bears this pain and carries the responsibility of doing what he can to bring this richness alive in his own tradition. He also must serve as a bridge person between the traditions. This is a great task, for it implies that he not only enter in depth into his own tradition so that he can understand it well and present it as experienced, but also that he enter as deeply as he can into the other tradition, so he can both bring its riches back to his own tradition and help his fellows understand and accept them, and at the same time understand how best to bring the riches of his own tradition sympathetically and humbly to the other tradition.

Rarely can one enter with fullness into a tradition that is not his own. Attempts to do so usually lead to a certain amount of superficiality and lack of integration. But entering fully into his own tradition and becoming fully integrated, he can, depending on his depth, meet other traditions with an openness and depth that can even surpass that of persons within the other tradition who have not the same depth.

Great spiritual masters of the East have told me that they have rarely found anyone who understood them so profoundly as Merton, but Merton in his practice was totally Western Christian and Cistercian, though with an extraordinary depth.

*   *   *

In the reading at Vigils this morning, Isaac of Stella asserted, "When all are united with God they become one God." At first blush the statement could be taken as being quite literally pantheistic. Isaac goes on to explain: "The Son of God is one with God by nature; the Son of Man is one with him in person; we, his body, are one with him sacramentally. . . . What Christ is by his nature we are as his partners; what he is of himself in all fullness, we are as participants. Finally, what the Son of God is by generation, his members are by adoption."

Sometimes the statements made by our Eastern brethren incite us to cry, "Pantheism!" But perhaps if we listen to them carefully and try to understand what they are really saying, we will discover that, without the help of the Christian Revelation, and with very different thought patterns and philosophical concepts, they are trying to express the same Reality as our mystics, which they have perceived through their own mystical experience and contact with a tradition that goes back to the primitive revelation.

Isaac tells us that what he affirms "is the explanation of the Lord's words: 'Father, I desire that as you and I are one, so they may be one with us.'" I think we find it difficult, indeed impossible, to grasp the fullness of the Lord's statement—to be one with God as the Son is one with the Father! Can any greater unity be conceived? The mode or manner of unity is different, we rightly assert, but the reality is an incomprehensible oneness.

In sharing with our brothers and sisters from the East, we need to depend very much on the native Christian leadership who are familiar with the way their tradition thinks and speaks and let them help us interpret and understand what is being said. We will, I think, find the authentic spiritual masters striving, like some of our own mystics, to speak of a mystical experience of God and even of an intuition of the Trinity, but necessarily relating it with their own traditional modes of expression. Hearing these realities spoken of in quite different ways can invite us to new, enlivening perceptions of them.

Herein, it seems to me, lies one of the great values of dialogue beyond the confines of the Christian churches and communities. To collaborate in building a solid spiritual base for the global family is important. The quality of our own individual lives and the degree of our entrance into the divine life will determine the significance of our contribution. This, indeed, holds good for all we seek to accomplish in life.

*

To see God is to be God.

—Thomas Keating

*   *   *

Into the fourth day of retreat. I found myself this morning asking how it was going and evaluating it by what I "got done"—that productive ethos still clings. I don't need to get anything done these days—or ever—except what he wants me to do, and right now he simply wants me to be and rest in his mercy.

*

Life is like the sunset: some days it is absolutely magnificent—like this evening when all the shades of red filled the sky and the lake was dancing crimson—other days the sun just drops into the sea and all is black.

*   *   *

The retreat is over. What did I get out of it? (There I go again!) A deeper realization of some fundamentals:

- Thoughts, ideas are not what is wanted—but experience.
- God is really beyond—yet all—one is good—all that is and that is good is God—we really need incarnation.
- God is in this instant, no other—full presence, die to self by being wholly alive to the reality of the instant—but we do not really lose ourselves because we find self-being in that Reality—resurrection.
- I am very lazy—not willing to make the effort with any constancy to respond to the deeper reality—then failing in respect and reverence most of the time—doing very little real praying.
- Too creature-comfort oriented—afraid to push myself. "When you wear shoes the soles grow thin; when you go barefoot the soles grow thick."

I need to clear some clutter out of my life and spend more time doing the one thing necessary—really seeking God.

*   *   *

Interviewer: What are you bucking for?

Peter Grace: I just want to be able to look the Lord in the face and say I did everything I should have done

that day to protect the interests of many thousands of
people who depend on me.

——*Chemical World*

*   *   *

What would our spirits be, O God, if they did not have
the bread of earthly things to nourish them, the wine
of created beauties to intoxicate them and the con-
flicts of human life to fortify them?

*

A man has to be able to do something with his feelings
and ideas, he has to try to give them to somebody and
try to share his own understanding of himself and life.

——Teilhard de Chardin

*

Homo sum, humani nihil a me alienum puto.

——Terence

*   *   *

"Go forth to the whole world."

This is usually considered horizontally, to cover all the
face of the globe. The monk's call is to do this in spirit and care.
But he must not restrict himself to the horizontal level. He
must seek to go to the height and the depth, to transform all
consciousness, till Christ is truly all in all.

*   *   *

Your life is hidden with Christ in God. When Christ
who is our life appears, then you also will appear with
him in glory.

——Colossians 3:3

As Saint John tells us in his Prologue, all created things were living in Christ, the Word, through all eternity, and in the course of time were made through him. If this is true of our natural life, it is even truer of our special participation in Divine Life through elevating and illuminating grace. This life of ours in grace still remains very hidden in Christ in God. When finally Christ is fully manifested in the day of his glorious coming, the fullness of our own life will be manifested, though, like his and because it is a participation of his, never fully comprehended. For it is a participation in the Divine Life itself.

But even now on the journey we can begin to receive some intimation of the glory of our full life in God, if we want it. This is what we experience in deep prayer when we enter into ourselves, going to our very center, beyond all thoughts and images, and pass through our center into the center of God, the ground of our being, the constantly present and active creative Source. "Be still and know that I am God." In the deep inner silence God manifests himself, his Christ, and ourselves to ourselves. For when God is manifested to us we see ourselves as we truly are, in him. This is the only way we can get in touch with and perceive our true selves, the glorious being that we are—partakers of Divine Life and Being.

How foolish we are to identify so much with the poor superficial image we behold in the mirror, or the concocted image we carry in our imagination, or the distorted images we see reflected back at us from others, even our best friends or surest guides. We need to perceive the undistorted image, and this we can do only in deep prayer, when we look into the "eyes" of God in love and see ourselves reflected back in his creative love. We are so beautiful that if God let us see our true beauty anyplace but in him we would succumb to idolatry. In him we know our true nothingness of ourselves and our allness in him.

How wonderful it is to be the beloved of God!
"All for the praise of the glory of his grace . . . in the Beloved."

——Ephesians 1:6

*

When we know or perceive things or even persons only in themselves, we know them only as very fragile realities that can slip away from us so easily. At any moment our prized possession may break, be stolen, be lost, be used up, or our friend may die or go away, or we may ourselves die and lose them all. But when we know and possess and enjoy things and persons in God then we know them in their eternal and unextinguishable reality. We can never lose them and always enjoy them to the full in all their beauty, a beauty that is a participation of the divine beauty, life, being.

Yesterday we received word that Brother Louis died. It came upon us with a certain swiftness. His brain tumor was discovered only a week or so ago. Now he is gone. But not gone. For we know Louis in the Lord. He is still much alive, more alive than ever, and very present to us. "Life is not ended, but changed" (Preface of the Funeral Mass). Before, he was far away in our daughter house in Azul; now he is very close. Indeed, even when he was far away in Azul, he was very close, because we knew him and cherished him in the Lord.

Life is so different when it is lived at this level of faith and insight. As Saint Paul puts it: "Possessing nothing, but having all things." Instead of greedily grasping what little of life there is within our immediate reach, we let go, enter into God, and in him find all things and persons in their fullness and enjoy them in their fullness. Far from denying the beauty and goodness and value of created things and persons, this detachment from grasping, materialistic possessiveness allows us to experience and affirm the eternal and participatively divine value, goodness, and beauty of each thing and each person.

What a precious gift is faith and the insights of faith! Yesterday was the World Day of Prayer for Vocations. In gratitude for the gift that is ours in faith, how earnestly we should pray for vocations. "Pray therefore that the Lord of the harvest will send laborers." Faith comes through hearing. Knowing what our faith means in our own lives, and loving our brothers and sisters, we cannot but long that they, too, might receive this most precious and beautiful gift; that the Lord would raise up many ministers of the Word to bring the gift of faith to those who do not yet share this life-giving and elevating insight.

If the light of the Resurrection did not shine in our lives and deaths!

May Louis rest in peace and enter into the fullness of the divine glory. We will sing the community Mass for him this morning. Then each of the priests will offer three more Masses for him in the coming days as we consecrate thirty days of special prayer for him—and for all who love him, especially his dear sister and all the brethren at Azul.

*   *   *

One beggar tells another where to find bread. Men keep coming; today I expect ten. The last two weeks have been as busy as any. For a good number it is just that—giving them a bit of the Bread of Life in one form or another—love, affirmation, a word from Scripture, a bit of rest, a time and space to breathe a little more deeply. But for some it is the beginning of an ongoing relationship, even the beginning of a life.

If I sit back and reflect, I sense a fear arising of being wholly consumed, broken into many pieces, the food for too many. But as I move quietly through it, the food seems to come from an inexhaustible supply deep within, that I get in touch with and invite others to get in touch with as we repeatedly sit together in Centering Prayer. It is good.

*

The valleys are filled with mist. It is cooler and quieter down there. It is like descending into centering—cool, quiet, restful, a place it is good to be, a source of living water that vitalizes the surroundings, a constant invitation, an obscurity, a peace.

The bell for Lauds will ring in a moment, filling the surrounding valleys with its solemn joy. Some days I wait for it, my whole being wanting to laud our wonderful God. It is good to be able to enter into the community's praise, the Church's praise, the creation's praise—my own is so inadequate—nothing is adequate except the Holy Spirit.

*   *   *

There goes the bell—the Bell of the Virgin, or, rather, Saint Bernard's bell—deeper, sharper than the Bell of the Virgin—rather like Bernard must have been, the great prophet crying out and commanding all Christendom, calling droves of men to cloister and crusade. I don't find him particularly attractive—perhaps it is because I don't know him well enough—but rather an awesome person.

At Holy Trinity Monastery

Dana came late Friday night. Friday was a busy day, getting everything together for the journey and finishing up things. Saturday was more packing, with time out to plant tulips. Our sheepdog had gotten into the bulbs and scattered them, so it was necessary to take time with them.

We got off around ten—a bright, beautiful spring day. We reached Auriesville around 1:30 and spent an hour or so in prayer, visiting the shrine of the North American Martyrs.

We got to Jordanville around three. We had no difficulty finding the monastery. The church is a splendid example of Russian Orthodox architecture, and seems almost unreal in the New York countryside. It is dedicated to the Most Holy Trinity.

Father Serafim was warm in his welcome. It turns out he is a Cuban. He grew up with little faith, was awakened by Buddhism, as was his mother, and then became a Roman Catholic and an Eastern Rite Benedictine. After a while he dropped out. Finally he found his way to Orthodoxy a couple years ago. He is a busy, gossipy man. He translates, edits *Orthodox Life,* and works in the barn like everybody else—they have sixty cows under milk. It is a very busy place, with a big farm, a theologate for about fifty students, and a printing press. It is the only flourishing monastery and printing works in the Synodal Church.

There is a tremendous difference since my last visit, when they were almost all old emigrees. Now there are a number of middle-aged and young monks, and ten novices. This has done wonders for their singing.

There was little Vespers, Compline, Akathist and Canons of Preparation from 4:00 to 5:30. Then supper—cabbage soup, potatoes, noodles, coffee, bread. Father Seraphim, a rather ample man, made much of their fasting and the poor plainness of their food. But Dana, a cook, thought it was very good. I found it equal to ours.

At 7:00 the Vigil began. It was magnificently done, with a very full church. Bishop Laurin, the Hegumen, presided in magnificent cloth of silver. It lasted about three and a half hours. We spoke with Serafim till 11:30, then lost an hour with daylight saving time coming in. All was sung in Old Slavonic. Many of the old monks know no English. But many of the young are looking to the time when services will be in English.

Father Serafim has a very negative view of the world, and especially of his native Cuba. He has "washed his hands of it all" (said with an expressive gesture). He feels this is what opens men to God's call; men must come to the monastery to find God—nothing else. He emphasized the sobriety of Russian monasticism—though he often broke out into a rather loud laugh. He centers on the suffering Christ even during the Paschal time.

It rained heavily during the Vigil but now it promises to be a beautiful spring day. I just woke Dana and we will soon be on our way. It would have been nice to be here for the baptism at eight and Pontifical Liturgy at nine. But we had a good bit of services last night and ecumenical sharing, so I decided we would move on. I could spend my whole life just moving about, sharing with monks and lay people of all faiths who are eager for this. It would be a hard life. It is difficult to really settle into deep prayer at strange Services. Through the long Service last night I felt I was doing very little real praying. Too much attention has to be given to the situation.

*			*			*

At Genesee Abbey

Most of yesterday was cloudy, but no rain. We left Jordan-ville at 6:30 and arrived at Genesee Abbey around 5:30 in the evening. I had a good talk with Abbot John Eudes, then Compline, and then a talk with Father Stephen. This morning we had Vigils at 2:25. I said Mass after Vigils for the hermit Brother Elias and two others, since the community Mass is not till 4 P.M.

The monastery looks wonderful. The landscaping turned out very well. The old church is now a magnificent library. They have just built ten more rooms. The community numbers around forty, with seven in the novitiate. Father Francis is in Africa for a year or more as novice master, then Steve will go. Father Abraham is here, as is Father Henri Nouwen. The feel of this place is good. It is quieter in ways than Spencer. A sense of more control and discipline or structure comes through.

Everything is being redone in very good taste, yet not departing from simplicity. Poverty for monks is a difficult question. Saint Benedict said the monastery should be fully equipped. Beauty is supportive of contemplation. Yet we think of, feel with those who have to live in squalor and insecurity and real need. How do we relate with, speak to them? We give witness that if Christians bond together, sharing mutual support, all can have a decent life. We give what alms we can. We welcome all to our churches and guesthouses, to our membership. We pray for all the social and economic needs. Yet there is a feeling that this response is not adequate. But within the bounds of fidelity to our own vocation—what more can we do? It is an abiding concern.

Time for Lauds.

Returning from the Cistercian Conference

This year's conference was undoubtedly one of the best ever. For one thing, there was more space—because of shorter formal sessions—to enjoy the many friendships that have grown over the years. The conference is so completely interdisciplinary, but much more. It relates with every dimension of life.

The Benedictine Sesquimillennium brought a goodly number of nuns and monks. The Vespers and love feast at St. Gregory's Abbey seemed to be a culmination of the relation begun ten years ago at the first conference. It was a joy to see the community flourishing with many young members. The Anglican presence at the conference was strong and enriching.

Sister Benedicta Ward gave the keynote address on the miracles of Saint Benedict from the Fleury tradition—quite different from the Monte Cassino and Roman outlook. The liturgies were very good and the turnout and presence at the prayer workshop was far beyond all expectation. The evening of sharing on Cistercian life today was a natural culmination of the Cistercian program. The presentation of samplings from eight centuries of Cistercian music, offered at the Presbyterian church downtown, the exposition of the many medieval manuscripts of the Rule of Saint Benedict at the Cistercian Institute Library, the slide presentation of Cistercian monasteries old and new—each added its own dimension.

The sessions and discussion on comparative mysticism along with the visit to the ashram in Fennville brought a new global expanse to the conference which I experienced as especially rich and a further part of my preparation for India. In these sessions our abbots and spiritual fathers and Eastern masters were able to make the contribution proper to them more readily than in the academic sessions.

The time with Jim, touching base with family doings, and with Matt and Dennis and other candidates, added its own immense joy and richness to the overall experience. Great weather, the first glorious days of spring, invigorated the whole.

It was a joy to see Cistercian Publications coming into its own with a very successful year. Rozanne has done a great job on so many levels of activity. I am very grateful to the Lord for so much.

As Jim and I waited for the plane, we reflected on the years past. How impossible it would have been for us even to have imagined thirty years ago when we were together in college that we would ever have such a sharing in Kalamazoo, the fruit of so many happenings, the wondrous unfolding of a loving Providence in our lives.

And now, what next? In many ways, things seem to be coming to a conclusion for me. I look forward more and more to India. I want to do a good bit of reading and reflecting and praying to prepare for it. I suspect it will be a very significant and perhaps traumatic experience. Father Thomas Davis said to be prepared for the worst and it will be worse still. He said it took him all of a year and more to integrate his experience there. It was only on Mount Athos that this came to completion for him. The fact that I have already spent a good bit of time on the Holy Mountain may be of help. I expect that the spiritual sharing will be very rich, but the poverty, and even more the indifference to it, very disturbing. It is one thing to hear about poverty, another thing to be immersed in it, as it were inescapably. Add to this sounds and smells and tastes and sights that are so different from a lifetime's experience of familiarity ... Even now as I fly from Kalamazoo, there is a very good feeling about going home. I love Spencer very much. As wonderful as the conference was this year and as much as I enjoyed the beautiful people there, there is always the sensation of being out of my proper environment. How profoundly this will be experienced in India! While I am sure monastic hospitality and fraternity will bridge many gaps and be very supportive, I am going to rely a lot on meditation and prayer.

*

We sail now breathlessly through empty skies. Like the emptiness of enlightenment or the mysticism of Eckhardt, it is full—full of sunlight and warmth, imparting vigor and life. We spent a lot of time this morning at the East-West dialogue trying to express the unexpressible, and sensed, more than judged, that we were in fact all ultimately struggling to speak of the same unspeakable. Undoubtedly there are levels of experience as to duration and quality and intensification. The diverse development of consciousness in our respective traditions gives us varying abilities or facilities in relating our experience and its after-effects. We seem to use a lot of words to try to say what cannot be said. We seek symbols that can convey what we cannot say.

*   *   *

Mixed feelings:
A little tired—the end of a day. A good feeling that I am kind of caught up on things and can settle into a more contemplative pace. Yet there is something in me not so eager to slow down, that likes the go-go. But it will quiet. I feel the need of more space and quiet to do more prayer and deeper thinking. I feel surfaced, spread out, thin, not able to speak words of life.

In a way I feel very much one with, involved, knowing in a live way, conscious of presence. I can close my eyes and I am there.

Into your hands I commend my spirit—and all.

*

The birds are singing wildly—too enthusiastically for such a heavy muggy morning. The haze hides the sunrise. It promises to be an uncomfortable day.

It is good to be back in rhythm, up at three. The day seems out of kilter and somewhat lost when the early hours are lost to sleep.

It will be a busy day. The novice master of Glastonbury and his novices are coming for the day. And Ray is coming this evening. I am very happy about Ray. He is such a beautiful young priest. He will bring so much to the community.

I wonder sometimes if I should not take a stricter line in some areas with the candidates. Do I challenge them enough? We all tend to cut corners in different ways. We need to be really honest with ourselves, admit and accept our weaknesses, without making them a major hassle. If we seek the fullness positively, some things will fall away. I think that is the right approach, rather than concentrating on the weaknesses, which can only make them more of a stumbling block. We should try to see what is behind a particular weakness: why a fellow is short-fused or feels depressed and compensates with overeating, or masturbating, or drink, etc. I myself tend to overeat or at least eat more than I really need, and this keeps me on the heavy side. Why? Partly it is probably just a bad habit; having to sit through a long silent community meal with nothing else to do but eat doesn't help. Supper brings one of the few chances to socialize with the brethren—also the coffee breaks. But at times it is compensation, or just indulging a desire for some sense pleasure—especially when I eat between meals.

*   *   *

The things of God are to be suffered, not to be learned.
——Archimandrite Ponteleimon

Yesterday Brother Damian, who is to be consecrated a monk on the feast of the Visitation, and I visited the monastery of the Holy Transfiguration in Brookline. We had a couple very beautiful hours with the Elder, Archimandrite Ponteleimon. Father was most gracious and warm in his reception. There were no polemics, though Father told me he would have preferred my not having written about him in my last book. He experiences particular attacks from the evil one when others praise him. Father now lives much of his week in a small monastery on the rocky coast of Maine, where a group engages in translation work. They have completed the writings of Isaac the Syrian and other ancient monastic Fathers, including John the Solitary. They are also working on a translation of the New Testament, depending on the commentaries of Saint Nicodemus of the Holy Mountain to elucidate difficult passages. Father shared many delightful tales of the monastic saints with us in the course of our conversation.

Damian sought a word of life and Father gave him this (after protesting that he was not one to speak about sublime things—it is better to abide in silence): "The things of God are to be suffered, not to be learned." God and the things of God are to be known, not by study and reading, but by experience. This, Father said, is why prayer is so hard. In prayer we experience God, and, in that Light, our own sinfulness and evil and darkness. It is very painful to persevere in prayer.

Father looks well. His beard is just beginning to turn gray.

His hearing is failing a bit. As we prepared to leave he asked us each to choose an icon from among their rich collection. Damian chose his holy patron. Father gave him the icon and then said he must choose another because he had to choose his patron; he should choose one that will call him to compunction. Damian then chose the icon of the holy Mother of God called "Quick to Hear." Father said that was his favorite icon of the All Holy One. It is on the screen in their chapel. I chose a detail of an icon by Kontaglou, a head of Christ, which portrays him looking reproachfully at Saint Peter after Peter had denied the Lord. It will indeed call me to compunction as I, like Peter, so often fail the Lord and do not live up to what I have promised him. Father also gave us boxes of their incense to burn in our chapel. It was a most gracious and grace-filled visit. Much suffering, which Father has had these past few years, has fashioned a most gentle and wise Father. Besides the thirty-seven monks at Holy Transfiguration, and the small community in Maine, Father has a convent of nuns in Jamaica Plains and a large convent on an island in the Aegean. Blessed are they all in such a Father!

*   *   *

In the end, to choose the Church is an act of faith.
———Fulton Sheen

*   *   *

Ascension Thursday

In the recent past, it seems to me, we tended to be somewhat fixated on Calvary. The Passion, the Cross, suffering, a painful, self-denying following of Christ seemed to be central. These realities, of course, can never be left out of the picture. They are in their own way central. But I think a very important lesson bore in on me when I visited the great basilica in Jerusalem. I had to search for some time to find Calvary. It was all but hidden, off in a corner. Central and dominating the whole basilica was the empty tomb. Christ is risen. As Pope John Paul proclaimed in Harlem: "We are an

Easter people." We seem to forget that, forget that Christ spent only three hours on Calvary, only three days in the tomb, a gateway to a new risen life. We were baptized into the death and resurrection of Christ. We went down into the water and came up again. None of us was left in the baptismal font.

We are much more conscious now of the Easter Mystery, of the Risen Lord. But, again, we are in danger of stopping short. Christ rose and *ascended into heaven.* His sojourn was but forty days and nights. The beautiful anaphora of Saint John Chrysostom reminds us, as we pray to the Father:

From nothingness you called us into being; and when we had fallen away from you, you raised us up again, and you did not cease to do all things for us until you brought us back to heaven and endowed us with your kingdom which is to come.

Christ now lives in heaven. And we, because we have been baptized into Christ, live now in heaven, too, more truly than on earth. So Saint Paul tells us: "If you have risen with Christ, set your hearts on the things which are above, where Christ is seated at the right hand of God; seek the things that are above, not the things that are on earth."

We are an Easter people, but we are also an Ascension people. We are citizens of heaven.

*

We too are already in heaven with him, even though what he promised us has not yet been fulfilled in our bodies. Why do we on earth not strive to find rest with him in heaven even now, through the faith, hope, and love that unite us to him? ... In him, we can be there by love.

———Saint Augustine.

*

It is again a time of intense longing and desire. On the seven days preceding Christmas we end Vespers with the poignant cries of the "O Antiphons": O Wisdom . . . come and teach us; O Adonai . . . come and redeem us; O Root of Jesse . . . come and deliver us; O Key of David . . . come and lead us out of darkness; O Radiant Dawn . . . come and enlighten us; O King of the Nations . . . come and save the work of your creation; O Emmanuel . . . come and save us, O Lord, our God.

Now again, beginning with the Vespers of Ascension, we take up the same poignant melody, but the cry now is for the coming of the Spirit: Come, Father of the poor; Come, Giver of recompense; Come, Light of hearts. . . . O most blessed Light, fill our inmost hearts.

We abide, these days, in deeper prayer with Mary and the Eleven.

*　　　*　　　*

Sunday

> I pray that they may be one, Father, as you and I are one, that they may be one in us.
> ——Jesus (today's Gospel)

The World Monastic Council has been conducting an organizational meeting here and at Petersham this weekend. It is a fascinating and exciting group: Juliette Hollister, Founder of the Temple of Understanding and her successor Edward Bednar, Ewert Cousins, Director of the Spirituality Program at Fordham and Chairman of World Summit of Religions Meeting, Richard Payne, Editor of the Classics of Western Spirituality, Paulo Soleri, Architect of Arcosanti, Pope Coleman, City Planner for Cincinnati, representatives of the Association of Contemplative Sisters, Gordon Schultz of the World Council of Churches, Lex Hixon, who does New York radio and TV shows on spiritualities, and many others. A seed has been sown. How it will develop remains to be seen. If all exercise the creative enthusiasm of Juliette Hollister, and the humor, it will be a smashing success. Its goal: to bring all monastic and similar spiritual currents in the great traditions into unifying dialogue and experience of each other.

Monasticism is a rather visible archetype of a basic humanizing and divinizing dimension of the human person and society. As institution it is one of the oldest, most perduring and universal in the world. While some religious cultures feel uncomfortable with or even strongly reject the label "monastic," it can be seen to have meaning even for them. Protestants are slowly and quietly refinding this part of the Christian heritage, even Luther's own followers. There are Lutheran Benedictines in Sweden and the United States. The Episcopalians have numerous monastic houses now. Taizé is world-renowned. And there are many other more quiet experiments as well as significant bodies that represent monastic living. Among Islam there are the Sufi, married like the Jewish Hasidim, with marked monastic traits. Buber has pointed out the four characteristics or "virtues" cultivated in Hasidic communities and they are the very ones fundamental in Cistercian communities.

1. *hitlahavut:* the fire of ecstasy—a sense of having tasted God, of having in some way anticipated the *joy* of heaven.
2. *avoda:* work or service—a constant effort to let creation ascend to God, to live a life that is properly in focus.
3. *kavana:* singlemindedness, inner devotion, directing all to God.
4. *shiflut:* humility in the knowledge of oneself as part of a community, complementary to others—being truly oneself.

It is hoped that interaction among the masters of these various institutional expressions of the human person's most transcending ideals will help bring into existence that global spiritual base for an ethical and even affective human society, as well as throw light on innumerable facets of life: holistic education of children, food, sleep, rules for life, small industries, ecological environment, pharmacology, meditation techniques, dying, etc.

*

My dear brothers, we are already one. But we imag-
ine we are not. And what we have to recover is our
original unity. What we have to be is what we are.

——Thomas Merton

*

But ideas sometimes slip into the world as gently as
doves. If we listen attentively we may hear the gentle
flutter of wings ... nourished by millions of individuals, each and every person on the foundation of his
own inner suffering and joy is building for all.

——Camus

*

Now is the time so to act as to prove that God's height
does not lessen man's stature.

*

Unless you have the instrument, you are not going to
play the music. The environment is one of our instruments.

——Paulo Soleri

*

Convergence does not mean homogenization.

*

The new age is going to be as different from civilization as civilization is from savagery.

——Pope Coleman

*

The human condition is cast in institutions. We cannot
function without them.

*

Monasticism is the toughest, oldest form of religious institution in the world—a grass-roots institution.

——Ewert Cousins

*

Monastic hospitality means an open heart to all peoples. This means we need to learn how to be hospitable to all traditions.

*

"Service unites, doctrine divides" is a very superficial dictum. What motivates the service? Doctrine!

*

We die on the day our lives cease to be enlivened by a wonder beyond all reason.

*

Bernie Glassman, a Jewish man from Brooklyn, has received the dharma succession from a Zen master and has just established a dharma hall in New York, which he has dedicated to all true spiritual masters, especially those of the traditions of Shakamuni and Jesus. The study program there, directed by an American convert to Islam, places primary emphasis on oral *lectio divina* in the Jewish and medieval Christian style.

*

In our time it is more important to emphasize what unites rather than what divides.

——Pope John XXIII

*

Energy comes from servant leaderships.

*

Every person has something important to say, if only
someone has the patience to listen.

*   *   *

We had a gala evening, a cake and ice cream party in the
solarium, to honor "Uncle" Alf's eighty-eighth birthday and
Brother Tom's sixty-ninth, and to welcome home Father William from our daughter house in Snowmass, Father Kizito
from Gethsemani, Brother Mauro from Union Priory, and Father Robert Kevin from his hermitage in Norway. Uncle Alf's
remarks were full of thanksgiving, as were Tom's, adding:
"Persevere, persevere, persevere!" Father Robert is seeking to
discern if he should respond to the urgent and oft-repeated
pleas of the Bolivian bishops for a contemplative presence in
their country. He has spent twelve years in the cold dark
recesses of Norway. Maybe it is time to dance in the sun. He is
certainly a joyful person, still pink-cheeked and looking a bit of
an elf, especially with the colorful pointed hat of the Alta-plana
Campascino. His departure, it seems to me, would be a loss for
Norway. When I visited him there I found that almost everyone was conscious of his presence. It called a whole nation, as it
were, to something higher. In the primitive culture such as he
would settle into in the Bolivian highlands his presence would
be far less felt. But it might open out to these simple people a
dimension of the Church that would be very winning to them.
It is difficult to judge humanly where his presence would be
more advantageous. It calls for a listening to the guiding Spirit.
His ways are often not ours. To fulfill his primary task, it makes
little difference where the monk is situated, as long as he can
be free from those things that might impede him. It is his love,
or even more his openness to the Spirit of Love acting in and
through him, that leavens the whole of the created project and
directs it more surely toward its true meaning and goal.

*   *   *

"Do you love me more than these?"

So often I find my thought and attention taken up with the practical plans of life, far more than is really necessary. Then the Lord comes along and says: "Do you love me more than these?" "Yes, indeed, Lord, I do!" And he replies: "Feed my lambs." How? First of all, by love, by prayer, by being a channel of the graces that will feed and nourish their souls. By holding them up to the Divine Shepherd, who feeds them with his own flesh and blood.

Then, perhaps, also, I am meant to feed his sheep by my writing—to give more time to thought and prayer in view of being able to write of him in a way that will feed the minds and hearts of his lambs. Figuring out practical things where there is immediate hope of seeing results seems to be so much more gratifying or at least enticing, than deeper thought, penetrating into the divine Reality and Mysteries. I enter the cell of the heart, and instead of abiding there in the silence and emptiness, awaiting the knock and entrance of the Divine Guest, I am tempted to get busy and start furnishing the cell or rearranging the furnishings already there. But it is in the silence and quietness that I can hear him speak, learn from my Master, and have some nourishing food to share with his sheep. I need to experience my emptiness, my hunger—so that I can be myself fed by the Shepherd of Life.

THE PENTECOSTAL SPIRIT

Listen for the voice of the Spirit,
for that which enlarges the mind,
frees the heart, brings together
what was scattered and lost,
holds fast in unswerving fidelity,
instils peace, renews confidence,
comforts and endures. Happy are
you if you hear that voice!

Carrin Dunne

Pentecost

"The days of Pentecost are complete . . ."

It is hard to believe that fifty days have already passed
since we followed the Paschal candle down the cloisters from
the new fire into the dark church, and watched its spreading
flame dispel the darkness, giving cause to sing the *Exultet:* "O
Blessed Night, O truly Blessed Night!"

The Divine Seed was sown and now the first fruits come
forth—the renewing Spirit enlivens our spirits. In God's "all-
now" the water gushing from the side of the Crucified Corpse,
the breath of the Risen Christ—"He breathed on them and
said: 'Receive the Holy Spirit' " (John 20:22)—the outpouring
of the Spirit at Pentecost, and our Baptism are all one. In that
moment our spirits are enlivened with eternal and divine
life—the first fruits of Christ's saving mission. At the resurrection, our bodies, too, will be enlivened and divinized—then
the harvest will be complete.

*

Let anyone who is thirsty come and drink. Living
waters will flow from within him, alleluia.
——Response, Second Nocturn

*

107

On the last and greatest day of the festival [The days of Pentecost are complete. This is the last and greatest day of the Paschal Feast] Jesus stood there and cried out:

"If any man is thirsty, let him come to me!
Let the man come and drink, who believes in me!"

As scripture says: "From his heart shall flow fountains of living water." [When Christ died on the Cross, water flowed out from his pierced side—the outpouring of the Spirit.] He was speaking of the Spirit which those who believed in him were to receive.

——Today's Gospel (John 7:37–39)

Christ *gives* us his Spirit. The Spirit is *Gift* to us. He truly becomes *our* Spirit. This means I possess the Holy Spirit as my own Spirit—the full consequence of my having been baptized into Christ, the Son. With Christ, in Christ, as Christ the Son, I, too, can breathe forth the Spirit who is Love as a wholly adequate response to the Father and his great, his infinite love for me, his son. I can love God with an infinite love, with Divine Love. This realization is a great consolation for me, as it must be for any Christian, oppressed by so much personal sin and misery, standing in the face of infinite goodness and unending, infinitely patient love—*Quid retribuam Domino pro omnibus quae retribuit mihi?* What can I return to the Lord for all he has given to me? Thanks to Jesus, who, with the Father, this day sends forth his Spirit, and gives him to me as *Gift*, I can return to the Lord an equal, a divine Love. Amen. Alleluia!

*   *   *

Like dry flour, which cannot become one lump of dough, one loaf of bread, without moisture, we who are many could not become one in Christ Jesus without the water that comes down from heaven ... through the Spirit we have become one in soul.

——Saint Irenaeus

*   *   *

We need to foster communion in the lived experience of common spiritual values and the mutual confidence such an experience inspires. Let us recognize what unites us in the Holy Spirit. It will help if we can clarify the content of the life experience which we all share.

*   *   *

Our Lord said the one unforgivable sin is blasphemy against the Holy Spirit. He said this when people were attributing the good coming from him to the evil spirit. When we do not acknowledge the good that the Spirit is working in our own lives and in the lives of others, but see it as bad or defective, we are in our own little way (and sometimes big way) blaspheming against the Spirit. Nothing so blocks our spiritual growth as our refusal to recognize—with joy and gratitude—the good the Spirit is working in us, the effective presence of God's great love for us.

*   *   *

One can sense a certain excitement running through the house today. We are still under the mighty impulse of the Pentecostal Spirit. We look forward with expectation to the transcendent celebration of the Feast of the Trinity. Tomorrow is Mary's Visitation and we feel sure she will come and bring her Son and the prophetic Spirit into our midst. But most especially it is the eve of the consecration of a monk. In this a great grace is going to be poured out, not only on Damian, but upon us all, and upon the whole Church, the whole People of God. What an incredible thing when God espouses to himself in eternal nuptials a mere man! So complete is the binding that the man can never give himself to another in marital love, can never possess anything as his own. He is God's. And God is his! Truly can he say: *My* God! We will watch in the night in prayer with our brother as he prepares for this awesome moment—a moment that will last forever.

Trinity Sunday

Father Joe gave us a magnificent homily today—the powerful sharing of a holy man's experience of the Trinity.

The Feast of the Holy Trinity: This is the consummation of the liturgical year, of the life of the Church, of the Revelation, and of all Sacred History.

In the Garden of Eden God revealed something of his intimate love for his humans, but after the expulsion, that got shrouded in the mists of the passing centuries. Then he reached out to a chosen people and gradually descended from the fearsome grandeur of Sinai and a mysticism of dread, to speak again, through the prophets, of intimate love. And finally, in his Incarnation, he descended into the very midst of the human family and invited us again into his inner life. "I no longer call you servants, but friends, because I make known to you all that the Father has made known to me"—all that he is. But it is too much for us, so the Father and the Son send the Spirit to teach us from within. "You cannot understand this now. But the Spirit, the Paraclete, will come to you, and teach you all, everything that I have made known to you."

The Spirit has come and we have been baptized into the Son. The Spirit has come and he is now *our* Spirit. One with the Son, we cry, "Abba—Father," and respond to him with the Divine Love who is the Spirit—the wholly adequate response. This is our life now, the life of the whole Church. For the rest of the liturgical year, for the rest of the life of the Church, for the rest of Salvation History, this is what we do—what we are—till finally all comes to its ultimate fullness in the Omega—Christ Jesus, our Lord, until "all things are ours, and we are Christ's, and Christ is God's."

We move ahead now through the power of the love in the Sacred Heart, and its perfect reflection, the Immaculate Heart, through all the mysteries of the saints, and the unfolding of the creation, till we celebrate in time—at the end of the liturgical year—and in eternity, the glorious Kingship of Christ and our unending hymn of Thanksgiving.

Praised and blessed be the most holy and glorious Trinity, Father, Son, and Holy Spirit. Amen.

* * *

The sun is just capping a low bank of clouds, the air is fresh and cool, the birds are singing, the flow of traffic out on the highway comes as the murmur of flowing water. There is peace and quietness in it all. Three hours of the day are already gone, written for eternity. Father Joe stands in my thoughts. Life ended so suddenly, so capriciously—shot to death by a deranged person, yet: for those who love God, all things work together unto good. How passing earthly acclaim! Today he is a headline, a front-page picture; tomorrow only his boys will know his absence and many of them will soon enough forget for the most part. We are *very* little. Our only significance is in God and his plan—playing our little part, grateful for the gift of it, which is in fact something of infinite and unending beauty—but it is hard to keep hold constantly to that. To seek real meaning elsewhere is illusion.

*

A brother came last night. He had been far out and away from the sacraments five years. He told me the path back started last fall when he heard me talk. I remembered the conference, and how fruitless it had seemed to me. Praise the Lord!

*

My ministry to the young men is my joy now. Maybe there is a lot of self in it, and self-satisfaction of my natural attractions. But there is something wonderful—in the literal sense of the word—in being a part of a young man's finding himself and setting foot on a new, exciting, fuller life. God could easily use someone else, but he uses me. I am grateful, especially since my own life with its pleasure-seeking self-indulgence is hardly worthy of anything but reprimand. I don't seem to find the motivation or insight to make the effort to straighten out. It wouldn't involve all that much, but it just doesn't seem to be here. I will pray for it and try to think more of Jesus as my

Master, whom I totally accept and whose teaching is my norm. Lord, help!

*   *   *

A man can keep his sanity and stay alive as long as there is at least one person who is waiting for him.
——Henri Nouwen

*   *   *

Yesterday I spent the day in retreat. Reverend Father has given me permission to spend Wednesday in retreat. I went out after Compline on Tuesday and returned to say Mass at Compline time on Wednesday. Between bugs, heat, and headache, it was not an outstanding day. I realized my personal sensuality more, my need to discipline myself in mind and body, a terrible tendency to get constantly taken up in the details of life, and, above all, a too strong desire to be actively engaged in helping others spiritually, to have office and opportunity to do this. I found myself quite happy to have the day come to an end.

I take the resolve to try to mortify myself more constantly in little things; to try to build up the "cloud of forgetfulness" and enter more generously into the "cloud of unknowing"; to set aside all unnecessary practical and ambitious thoughts and to say a decade of the rosary in penance when I catch myself engaging in them.

Lord and Lady, help me! If I could but live the Indwelling!

*   *   *

I'm wondering if it might not be better for me to write these notes in the evening when my mind is more active, than in the morning when it is rather quiet. But I found that leaving it for the evening often meant omitting it as I was weary and ready for bed before I thought of it or got time for it. The day seems to gather its own momentum and become quite full, though that fullness includes prayer, meditation, reading, enjoying others, etc.

I don't feel pushed now, although there are many things waiting to be done. There are no real deadlines. I expect the summer to be quite full, with candidates, writing, other contacts, etc., but with a basic leisure about it. I have set up a couple of retreats which will give me even more space.

*

My mind has been wandering over a lot of practical plans: setting up my new room, refinishing the attic in the cottage, planning a book and a course on Saint Aelred. I like to work out practical things. There is perhaps a sense of accomplishment or power in organizing and arranging—a sense of productivity, getting things done, establishing order, etc. I have to watch that: the fascination of trifles obscures the good. I can fritter my time away on minutiae instead of doing serious and deeper creative writing.

*   *   *

A full and happy day. I feel very good. It is a bit warm—muggy, but not bad. A single bird still chirps as the sun—a great orange orb—sinks beyond the western horizon.

The cottage is full, with four beautiful young men. And Steve and Mike are due tomorrow. I got little done today. No matter. Being is enough. Wasting time with the Lord. I celebrated two liturgies—the second just for the joy of it, with three brothers in the Byzantine chapel.

There is a deep contentment. No push to do or even be more. Content to be as and where I am. Will the practicum on Wednesday put me in touch with some things I am not touching now? We are to talk of sexuality. I am comfortable with myself now. Happy about my body (though I could lose some weight), affectivity, attractions, etc. I am content with the friends and relations in the community. I don't really need others outside—but I am very grateful for them and enriched. There is more within than I can ever sufficiently exhaust. The turmoils, pains, needs, and pseudo-needs of the past seem remote. But I am sure others could come rushing in again, even though for the moment there seems to be such a sense of completeness and life in the ground of my being that I find it hard to believe it could be disturbed. We shall see. The Lord has his ways.

PEACE!

*   *   *

To fail to see the value of simply being with God and "doing nothing" is to miss the heart of Christianity.

——Dr. Leonard Doohan

*   *   *

A leisurely day, though some work done; interviewed two candidates (neither very promising). Quiet weekend in the cottage—two unpromising candidates—one promising candidate didn't show up. The week promises to be busy—a houseful of candidates, Mike and Steve for pictures, a Practicum, two council meetings. But no pressure. Happy about that.

Have been doing a lot of thinking about the foundation—perhaps too much. As I walked to Compline I was struck again by the beauty and really incredible creation Spencer Abbey is—again in church. We could never reproduce it in a foundation. It is a rare extravagance. Do I want to leave all I have here? No. And yes. Whatever I do, it has its pros and cons. It is good to feel I could be very happy staying here, just doing what I am doing or anything else—and I could be happy starting something new. Ultimately, it doesn't really matter. What matters? Something more indefinable than doing or being in a place. Connections are needed. But I feel confident I can establish them wherever I am. The deeper thing is a sense of wholeness, being, essential relation: a redeemed, saved sinner—comfortable with my sinfulness, somehow saved and related. Prayer seems to be constant, often surfacing verbally interiorly, but always there. More being than saying, even in the weakness and self-indulgence. God is very good.

I felt very good—still do—about a warm appreciative letter from Paris from the woman translating *O Holy Mountain* for Cerf. Sharing my weakness seems to have helped and touched many. How silly it is to put up a facade of strength and perfection. Yet I repeatedly try it. What a dope!

*   *   *

Thirty years of Cistercian life. For this I can never thank God enough. Certainly, there is much for which to be penitent. But I think all that can be forgotten—swallowed up in the fire of his Love. The reason for loving God is God; the measure, without measure.

*   *   *

Jude painted a wonderful picture of Saint Martin De Porres for my room. He said it took only five hours. What a genius! Saint Martin is arranging a bouquet in front of a statue of Mary. It is very colorful and unusual. I love it. Jude is so simple and gentle—one would never suspect he had such talents. I love him. Thank you, Lord, for Jude.

Vigil of Saint John the Baptist

We enter the feast of the Baptist. A monkey cactus, thorns in all directions, stands before the altar. How different my monastic life from his—how different in spirit—but at heart the same; at least this is my desire: a life wholly oriented to Jesus and pointing out the way to him to others, doing what little I can to prepare them to follow him. He was the first Christian vocation director, patron of our vocation chapel.

Pray for me, Saint John, *Agios Prodromos,* that I may be a good vocation father, that I may be a good monk of Christ, and more faithful to the ascetical life.

*

Joe comes on Wednesday or Thursday. I feel I should really invite him in. Ray called—arriving at 2 P.M. Monday. Thank God! Jim is also due Monday—beautiful Jimmy. And others coming, too. Gary on Thursday. Bob arrived today—an unexpected blessing. Lord, I love you and thank you for all.

*

The sun is gone. It is darkening—and chilling. Time to go in.

Feast of Saint John the Baptist

"He must increase and I must decrease."
——The Voice

If I want to communicate with someone, I have a word in my heart which I want to put into his heart. For that I normally need my voice. Yet the voice, once it has communicated the word to the other, needs to fall silent and disappear so the other can receive the word in the heart and attend to it and not be distracted by more voice. If I want to communicate Christ to others, he must be living in me. And once I have communicated him, I must disappear so that my brother can attend wholly to the Lord and not be distracted by my presence.

*   *   *

The Abbot gave an exceptionally full and good Chapter talk today before leaving for Berryville. The main theme: What do we want or expect from the visitation—what should it be in our times? From his experience, the visitor needs to arouse the community to special effort, make decisions in a short time of what are true issues, hear with equanimity (usually negative material is brought out first and then the positive that balances it). It is a time for planning for the 1980's: questions of energy, finances, numbers, a foundation. The Abbot said he plans on speaking on observance and exceptions, lest exceptions be taken as the new observance. He favors personal concern for each, making all the needed exceptions. He wants us to check in with him on exceptional things. Each is to spruce up his own observance, e.g., enclosure, eating between meals, getting to the Offices, getting to work on time, etc.

The visitation is a time for making a special effort to see what our Lord is asking of us today. We will prepare by hearings in community to surface what we see as the important issues. The visitor, seeing each monk, could surface other issues. Then there will be community dialogues on these. Then we will seek some clear statement of what has emerged and its practical consequences, if any, on how we are to move ahead.

*   *   *

The days disappear and I seem to accomplish nothing. I try to pray constantly but my prayer is very poor—often distracted. Be merciful to me, a sinner, Jesus!

Feast of the Sacred Heart

I preached the homily and was principal celebrant this morning. I felt I didn't have too good a grip on what I wanted to say, but I hope the Lord got said what he wanted said. Several spoke in praise of it and one said it was the "best yet"—but I don't know how much weight to put on that. It really doesn't matter, though; God and I are pleased with their kindness. I hope it means it has gotten to them.

We had a good quiet prayer meeting tonight.

*

I struggle a good bit with the idea of poverty, the very real needs of the poor and the expensive trip I am planning. I wonder if Tom Merton had any thoughts along this line when he planned his last trip. God has amply provided the means. It is hard to see clearly how much is truly according to his plan. We spend a lot on community celebrations. There is a certain fittingness, a place for beauty and celebration to his glory. Yet there is always the crying need of so many. How to balance all in true love?

*   *   *

This used to be the Feast of the Visitation. It was on this day in 1953 that Dom Edmund called me to make profession. I wonder what life would have been like if he had decided against it? There are so many crossroads and ifs in life. And always, no matter how invisible, the leading hand of Providence, so loving, so caring.

*   *   *

Father Malachy gave a wonderful homily. He quoted Freud: How a man spends his free time tells you what kind of man he is. Christ says the same: Where your heart is, there is your treasure. Father suggested one check his use of free time during the past three weeks. Father tied this in with the readings: Saint John's Last Supper discourse: "We will come and make our abode" with the first reading from Genesis: "Go into the land and dwell there"—an invitation to dwell in the land within. After we have finished our duties do we like to dwell within?

*   *   *

It has been a very busy week, with many in the cottage, and Dom Bede Griffith's visit. We finalized July 30th for Jim's entrance. There will be an advanced Centering Prayer workshop this week which should be quieter for me, though there will be a large group.

*   *   *

Days are disappearing so quickly. I have too many things to do. I hope I can learn not to take things on and to let things go, so I can really have some *otium sanctum* and do some real *lectio.* I saw the Abbot today and we talked about Transcendental Meditation as prayer and agreed completely—for the Christian or souls in grace it is contact with God and prayer. A natural preparation and then communication. But it must be practiced innocently, or it won't work.

*

The Hindu seems to say that the only reality is the transcendental experience (identifying the self with its consciousness) and the rest of our experience is illusion: the struggle with everyday things, including our own body and emotional needs. This really creates dualism: the real and the illusionary, that each must cope with. The Christian, accepting the true self and all his daily experience and doings as real, does away with duality. While accepting these things as real seems to introduce duality: God and non-God, in fact it functionally brings about in one's life a real unity. There is realized in the transcendental experience of God that while we and God remain essentially distinct, we are still very really one, a unity with personal distinction that in some way reflects the unity and trinity in God himself and enables us to share in his happiness of intersubjective or relational love. For this has he made us.

O Lord, our Master, how the majesty of your name fills all the earth! Your greatness is high above heaven itself.

*   *   *

We had a good discussion this evening on our "Cistercian method/technique." I hope and pray, and I fasted today, asking that the Spirit will come upon us in this, and a spiritual awakening will take place in all the community and the whole Order, beginning with myself. Lord, have mercy!

*

At most, methods are for beginners, and not even for all beginners.

——Louismet

*

There is general utility in the use of some methods in the spiritual life.

——Guibert

*

The Solemnity of Saint Benedict

I read the Prologue of the Rule and then renewed my vows. But I am far from living either. May the Lord help me to convert. I have lots of good intentions, but I don't get very far.

*

How do we stir up the Spirit? I guess we don't, for in today's prayer we ask the Lord to stir up within us the Spirit that set Saint Benedict on his course.

*   *   *

The Work of God for Saint Benedict is an *opus,* not a *labor.* God gives us the glory of letting him, in and through us, make it a great and glorious opus at the heart of his opus—the creation. The grace of the Benedictine vocation is to perceive this. The Benedictine monk is the one who prefers nothing to the Work of God. The ultimate meaning of the creation, of all that is, is the "praise of his glory." The work of the Work of God is to focus, sum up, direct the whole thrust, to give voice to the creation's cry of "Glory to God in the highest." And the result, the fruit we experience in ourselves and call down for all our brothers and sisters, is "Peace on Earth"—the tranquillity of order which ensues when all is ordered, as it ought to be, to God's glory. The power of the Work of God—the *Opus Dei*—to give focus to our lives and to the whole creation cannot be exaggerated—but it must be lived.

*   *   *

A quiet, but quietly busy day. I gave a class on the stages of spiritual growth, using Saint Aelred's Second Sermon for the Feast of Pentecost. I had to attend a Monastic Council meeting, which is a time-eater, but I say the Jesus Prayer during these meetings. I spend a half hour or so after Vigils each morning with the novices, saying the Jesus Prayer with the rope. I am a poor pray-er. I hope things will improve. They will, because God is good!

*   *   *

I sit here in the refectory, sipping coffee and eating peanut butter bread. It rained at last. We have been praying for it for days. It has been intensely hot and humid but the land has been parched. It is the worst humidity we have experienced in some years.

It has been, as I expected, a very busy time. We had a large workshop—advanced Centering—this past week. The flow of candidates is heavy. All kinds—at this moment a beautiful fellow just entering Norwich Military, a couple of jolly friars from the midwest, a thirty-six-year-old just out of prison, a thirty-four-year-old doing a master's in psychology, a member of the covenant community at Notre Dame, a potter from Minnesota.

*   *   *

The rains have come, after heavy hot days—they came in torrents just before Compline and continued through the night; an answer to prayer and a blessing—but not for all. Yesterday we dug a deep hole for the gas tank—now it is full of water. Also yesterday we started digging up the east road for resurfacing.

*

The heat and humidity have been difficult, but I feel better now. I am gradually moving into my new office. The new room is great. But I haven't really gotten into my schedule yet.

*

Modern thinking has undermined our convictions on the value of some mortifications, especially those inflicting pain, like the discipline, but even of fasting. I think we might safely let most of these go, *provided* we can accept the limitations that are necessary for other values. For example, limiting eating to the proper times for good order, to the proper quantity so as not to be weighed down, preventing clear thinking and freedom of the spirit; accepting the physical discomfort of a posture necessary to keep watchful and attentive at times of prayer. But the question that comes to my mind is: Can we successfully do these things if we do not go beyond them in some physical penances? If we really value penance, we will want to do more. If we do not value it, we will seek to cut corners even in those areas where we should deny our sensual desires.

I see the value of reducing sleep so that I will have more time for prayer, but I experience a certain drag on my positive psychological response which I think flows from the lack of sleep. The need is to find the minimum necessary. I tend to limit it perhaps too much and then need more. Is this a good way to function—cutting down and then occasionally taking a long sleep?

*   *   *

Sunday Aelred mentioned he wanted a better bed, so I offered him mine. Today he took it and I found the detachment something that cost even though I wasn't using the bed. Things get a hold on us.

Detachment: A freedom of the will whereby a man clings to or desires nothing for its own sake, avoids superfluity in his use of the goods of the earth and centers all of his attention, desire, and love on God, doing all else only for his sake.

——Dubay

*

I took a big box of books down to the librarian. He wasn't too happy about their arrival. I really didn't respond to his unhappiness with sympathy. Only after Compline did I get to think about them, and I took the books back.

*

Reverend Father came in to talk about some more work. The one job I find somewhat repugnant is the very one he had in mind. I had to laugh. The Lord sure has his ways. I told Reverend Father I would accept anything he wanted.

* * *

Cool, quiet; I am content.
I hope today to get into my new office substantially.

*

I decided to do Saint Bernard this year with the students. I still have a commitment to an Aelred paper for the Meeker's Festschrift. The candidates need a great deal of time, especially the correspondence. A new inquiry every day and a cottage almost always full. I am happy about it—but it precludes study and writing for the most part.

* * *

He spoke the word to them, so far as they were capable of understanding. He explained everything to his disciples when they were alone.
———Mark 4:33f

Jesus reveals God to us through the word proportionately to our capacity and desire. If we are truly his disciples and make time to be alone with him, he will explain all to us, he who is the Wisdom of God, he who knows everything. How foolish to let curiosity and an undisciplined desire of knowing squeeze the time alone with the Lord, as it sends us chasing after ephemeral knowledge in newspapers, periodicals, conversations, etc.

Saturday, Our Lady's Day

Mary, I so much need your help to be a worthy son of God.

It is cool, quiet. The birds are not singing yet. There is only the ubiquitous hum of a machine. We don't seem ever to be able to turn them all off: an exhaust fan, a refrigerator pump, an oil burner—something is always whirring in the silence. Even on Mount Athos the silence of the night was penetrated with the sound of the generator of Vatopedi. Does modern man ever hear silence, or have we so polluted our environment that the sounds of silence have gone from our world?

> "If even you hear the sound of the wind through the reeds, you are not yet in silence."
>
> ——Arsenias

Feast of Saint Mary Magdalen

I received the habit thirty years ago.

I find myself struggling with a future occasion of sin and not able simply to let it go, sort of hoping that it won't occur or God will handle the situation. But hanging on to it is hanging on to sin in some way, and it makes real prayer and *lectio* impossible, except for a prayer for mercy for a sinner. The matter should be past in a week or so, but it makes this whole time a parenthesis of death instead of a time of life and growth. How can I abide it? Yet I do. O Lord, mercy!

*

In the storms of life we sometimes have to act like the camel driver in the desert in the face of a sandstorm. He gets his camel down, gets behind it, covers himself with a blanket, and waits it out. Then he gets up, shakes off the sand, mounts his camel, and goes on. Some things can only be met by retiring into a time of solitude.

*

It is one thing to give up sin—another to give up the affection for sin.

*

Experiencing guilt is a sign that a person is good. He has high ideals. He admits he has failed. He has not given up his ideals, but squarely faces his failure and admits it. He need but repent, let go of his guilt, accept healing, and go on. Feeling guilty is a way of looking down on something we have done. And we cannot do that unless we have risen above it. Some failure is normal in a person trying to live up to a high ideal. Even the just man falls seven times a day.

The Good News is the coming of Christ to power to enable us to hear the Word of God and keep it.

*   *   *

Yesterday marked the thirtieth anniversary of my receiving the Cistercian habit (and Father Bernard's 80th anniversary of vows!).—I have in this a lot for which to grateful. How few in our times have received this grace to wear the habit this long. In spite of my many failures, I still desire to wear it and live up to all it traditionally stands for.

I am grateful it was a day in solitude. I don't know if much is really gained in a single day in solitude over a day of retreat in the community. Perhaps the change is good and the prayer more constant. But I appreciate community life—Cistercian community life, with its silence and ample *lectio* time, combined with the encouraging example of the brethren and our prayer together.

And the variation of manual labor. I have done little of this in the past months. The loss is my own, though I think the community gains by the example of a priest regularly at the common labor. It is an important part of Cistercian life and asceticism. It teaches us much and affords the occasion for very real prayer and reflection.

From this day of retreat I draw the resolve to really pray

the Psalms, and Office as a whole. It is foolish to be there just with many words and mentally to be elsewhere. Also, to really seek in my *lectio* the outlook of our Cistercian Fathers and try to live it in all. I have been giving more and more time to them and find it very fruitful.

I found this in a footnote in an unpublished manuscript of Saint Bernard: *Munda cor, exoccupa ex omnibus, esto monachus, i.e. singularis. Unum pete a Domino, hanc requira: vaca et vide qui Dominus Deus est.* (Cleanse your heart, free yourself from all, be a monk, that is, singleminded. Seek one thing from the Lord, this ask: make space in your life and see who the Lord God is.)

*   *   *

The meeting with the Franciscan capitulars today seemed to go off well. I spoke on the contemplative dimension of their life. At Mass I gave what for me was a surprisingly strong homily. I hope all its zeal was from the Lord. On the way home I stopped off to see the Little Brothers of Saint Francis at their *carceri*. I believe this little group bears an important charismatic witness, but they are getting tired of living constantly in such complete dependence and beginning to be tempted to seek more of this world's security. They need to hold fast to Saint Francis' definition of perfect joy. But I should be careful here. It is not for me to define the charism of any other person. May Saint Francis guide them!

*   *   *

Saint Anne's Day

The anniversary of my profession. The day has been so busy, I have hardly had time to pray. Grateful. But humbled that I have done so little in these years to become a monk. If the Lord spares me, I will make a real new start at trying to live a monk's life. Help me, O Lord!

I went to the blood bank with Matthew Joseph. A little celebration of laying down a pint of life to commemorate and renew in an incarnational symbol that laying down of profession.

*

The heat and humidity go on.
The visitation goes on.
We go on.

Praise our God!

*   *   *

My Birthday

Forty-eight today. Thank you, Lord, for the gift of life. In some ways it should be more the mother's celebration, for she completed successfully a long difficult process. For the child, the gift of life has already been long enjoyed (we might say our celebration of birthdays in some ways fosters the abortion mentality, denying fetal human life) and the greater gift of life will come some days hence at Baptism. At birth the baby experiences only his dependence and need more totally.

*

Mom called. She has been in the hospital again—a new pacemaker. A three-hour operation without anesthesia—really hard. She is a valiant woman. And to my thinking, a very holy woman, because she is a very loving woman. May the Lord be with her.

*   *   *

In the reading this morning at Vigils, Archbishop Anthony Bloom drew an analogy between bird-watching and contemplation:

Early morning is the best time.
One needs to be quiet, silent, relaxed, yet watchful
    and attentive.

Perhaps here is the difficulty with some of the Eastern methods. Some are relaxed but not watchful, not seeking, truly seeking God. Others are watchful but not relaxed. Christian contemplation, Centering Prayer, is both.

*   *   *

The community met last night for a dialogue on poverty. Two questions: Is the level of poverty at Spencer O.K.? If not, what can be done? The community—at least those present, about fifty-five—came out about fifty-fifty with contentment on the present observance of poverty, though most expressed ideas for improvement. It is difficult to know what to use as a norm for judging our level of poverty. By our affluent surroundings we live poorly enough. But in comparison with our brothers and sisters in the third and fourth world, we live in great luxury. Saint Benedict calls for a different kind of poverty than that sought by Saint Francis. Benedict's monastery was to be equipped to meet all the monks' needs, and the monks were to receive new clothing while the old was still good enough to give to the poor. He was more for a poverty of complete dependence on the heavenly Father, sacramentalized in the Abbot-Father, with great freedom for attention to contemplation and the things of God. Yet with the world grown so small it is not easy not to feel guilty eating well when starvation is close at hand. Yet not quite close enough, so that the complexities of economics make it quite difficult for us actually to share what we have and feed the poor.

*

Our real values have to have a *communal-symbolic expression,* for example, days of silence, times and places of silence, asserting the value we place on silence. How do we express today true evangelical poverty and solidarity with the poorest?

*

Anyone today who is not terribly confused, is not thinking straight.

——Clare Booth Luce

*

All radicalism tends to moderate in the face of affluence.

*   *   *

A stream hollows out the land when it flows; so the flow of temporal things erodes the conscience. Remain unaware of many things, neglect some more, and forget about some.

——Saint Bernard

*   *   *

We received a long letter from one of our guests decrying the ecological abuse of using toilet paper that has designs printed on it: it is a waste of time, money, talent, and resources, and as the paper decomposes it releases the poisonous dyes into the ecological system. I agree with the writer. But I think the Prior would respond that he can better employ his limited time on contemplative prayer, holding the terrible needs of the world before the Lord, rather than phoning around to dealers to find out where we can find undesigned toilet paper. And I would agree with him.

It must be the vocation of some to act as ecological watchdogs and keep after these abuses. And we as monks, as Christians, as humans, responsibly sharing this earth, should back them up. All should, each according to his own proper vocation. There is a question of balance. As monks we should seek to practice good stewardship in all that we use, to raise consciousness in this area and give a good example. But our primary contribution ever remains one of concerned prayer.

.   *   *   *

At Mass this morning, I was struck at how fortunate we are. The principal celebrant was from Vietnam. Among the concelebrants were a black man from Barbados, an Indian from Patna, and an Italian from Calabria, as well as men from all parts of the States and Canada. Monks are supposed to be universal men, reaching out in heart and caring to the whole globe. To have in our midst men from different continents, of different nations, races, colors, and ethnic groups constantly calls us to this realization. We are of the Church universal and for the Church universal. Like Christ, our Master, our love is to extend to the farthest corners of the earth. The black, the brown, the yellow, the white—and the red, a number of us are part Native American—are all our brothers, one with us in Christ. If all these can live together in intimate love and sharing in monastic community, why can they not live together throughout the world?

How much we need to hear the Gospel!

A TIME OF DEDICATION

Anniversary of the Consecration of the Abbey Church

In 1975, the Lord truly took possession of the church which we had built with so much labor and sacrifice back in 1952–1953, and worked through the years to clear of debt. Finally all was ready for the Church in the person of the Bishop to turn it over irrevocably to the Lord. And the Lord came amidst fire and smoke, song and *miserere,* saying:

> Here will I stay forever,
>   this is the house I have chosen.
> I will bless her virtues with riches,
>   provide her poor with food;
>   vest her priests with salvation
>   and her devout shall shout for joy.
>
> ——Psalm 132:14–16

We are the heirs of this promise. The Lord does dwell in our church, in our midst, blessing our prayerful gatherings and all our doings. He blesses us even with material goods, and here we must have care. The medievals had a saying: "Religion attracts wealth and wealth destroys religion."

Saint Robert's life story illustrates this, as does the history of the Order. We are in danger of being co-opted by American affluence. Certainly with our private rooms, their furnishings, our enriched diet, etc., we have, even in the years since the church was built, moved away from a poorer way of life toward affluence. May the Lord preserve us! The hard times that threaten America because of the oil shortage, etc., may be a great blessing, especially for the Christian and the monk who are called to live the mystery of poverty.

In some ways it sounds ridiculous to say that men vowed to a poor, humble way of life should have to worry about affluence when even in our own cities and our own country our brothers and sisters are suffering acutely from a lack of the basic necessities of life, and within our global village millions

133

are dying of hunger. Something is really off in all this. What can we do about it? Here is where we most acutely experience our poverty. We seem helpless in face of the economic inequities of our nation and our world. Our powerlessness to respond adequately to the situation which lies on our hearts like a burning weight prostrates us before the face of God. We cry in our silent pain that he who is almighty will forgive our sin and redress the disastrous effects of it. For much of the famine, hunger, and misery comes from our inability to work together and share what we have and be good stewards of the earth instead of greedy exploiters. Lord, be merciful to us sinners!

*   *   *

The proliferation of nuclear power gives little hope for humanity outside of a transformation of consciousness. There is hope for us only if mankind begins to view things from a new state of consciousness, which will alter his perceptions and establish a new common ground, a new "self-image" for humankind, one that will see the human wholeness and connectedness of everything. All will be perceived as one with the self in God, as realities of beauty and worth, so all will be respected and loved as the self, and self will be respected and loved. In such a frame the possibility of destructively using our power will disappear; rather, there will be a quest to use it creatively.

First Saturday of the Month

A day of reparation to the Immaculate Heart of Mary.

I am not sure how reparation can affect Mary in any way. Perhaps it can increase her accidental joy by our love being more pure and full and by helping to make the same true of others. I would like to live more in the presence of Mary. This would help especially with modesty, humility, and kindness in speech and thought. I should ask the Abbot more frequently if there is anything more I can be doing to help him or the community to serve its growth, fidelity, and renewal. I certainly want to be more loving in my response to the Abbot and to all, and more gentle. I should try to keep my suggestions to really significant matters and also my interventions in the dialogue groups, and try to bring out more what others are contributing.

*   *   *

The heat and humidity continue, so I do not really exercise and feel stiff, especially in my back, and somewhat lethargic.

*

The Abbot General answered questions for an hour last night, in a very open, compassionate, and humble way. He is a very good man. A good witness to Benedictine poverty. He makes do with very little.

*

I feel a bit pushed at the moment. The correspondence keeps ahead of me. I haven't really gotten started on the classes for the Fall yet. The manuscript on the Cistercian Fathers is not being touched. Material coming in is piling up. The refinishing of my desk is only partially completed. Other projects await attention, etc. Yet I can peacefully let things ride and respond to the present, which is to attend to the many candidates, pray, read, be. Praise to you, O Lord!

*   *   *

Much rain—heat—humidity
The Abbot General left last evening for the consecration of a church in Holland, Klaarland, and then on to Rome for a few days before going to Africa.

*   *   *

Feast of Saint John Vianney

I was baptized on Saint John's feast—but then it was on August 9th. He is an almost frightening person in the totality of his passion for Christ-God. I could use some of that passion. Pray for me, Saint John.

*   *   *

Archbishop Antony suggests we draw a picture of ourselves showing our tongue reaching out and entwining all our greedy desires, our ears stretching out to all we want to hear, our eyes to all our curiosity wants to see. We would see then how extroverted we are and how little of us remains within.

*

Why do you work for perishable food? Seek that which is eternal.

*

A bit cooler this morning. Retreat Sunday. Father Tom Fidelis of Conyers is here, returning from a year in Africa, where he helped at the foundation in Nigeria.

*   *   *

Transfiguration

Until a man has had the overwhelming experience of the simultaneous proximity and remoteness of Being, is it truly God whom he contemplates in his need? Is the "You" of his prayer truly addressed to God? Is there not a danger that he will stop at the mere reflection of reality which is mirrored in his soul or constructed in his mind?

——Abishiktananda

*

Jesus is the true light who enlightens every person who comes into this world. As God the Son totally illumined his human mind, so the radiance of Jesus flows out to shine in the mind and heart of everyone who will receive it. And in that light we will see Light and know truly ourselves and our God.

*

Man's being is derived from the innermost depths of God's Being, yet the mystery of his origin baffles his understanding, being a matter of love, grace, and perfect freedom.

——Abishiktananda

* * *

A breeze from the west has finally cooled things off and reduced the humidity. Father Fidelis spoke of Ahum and their terrible humidity and dust and bugs and scorpions, etc. Makes our lot seem pretty good. The lack of air conditioning and swimming here means when the humidity persists, as it has for over two weeks, there is no relief and it begins to sap one's strength and have other effects.

*

I am reading Leclercq's *Saint Bernard and the Cistercian Spirit.* He is a bit hard on Saint Bernard, going too far, I think, in relation to Abelard, but Leclercq has always been for the underdog.

*

A dog attacked our sheep yesterday and killed a lamb. Sheep are so defenseless and depend so much on the shepherd—like us.

* * *

It is even chilly this morning—quite a change! And a great full moon of magnificent splendor.

*

To truly seek God, to seek Jesus—that is the heart of the matter. But how practically, effectively, do we do it? How am I doing it? I feel sometimes as though I am simply caught up in carrying out duties and there is no thirsting quest informing my activity. Lord Jesus, Son of God, have mercy. Vitalize my life so that as I read, pray, communicate, work, I am truly seeking—and finding.

*   *   *

I experience a lot of concern over the candidates and their needs, and the decisions that have to be made: Should Dan move ahead now or wait a while? Should we reconsider Rob? Is Mike too hyper for our life? How to respond to Bill's desires for contemplative space? What to do about the non-candidates seeking space and attention in the cottage? I have to just let all these concerns sit quietly in my mind and heart and move along, trusting that the Spirit will help so that, in consultation with the Board and with the men, it will be clear. Lord, help us.

*   *   *

The Anniversary of Baptism

How can I ever be sufficiently grateful for this gift? Even writing this leaves me in confusion. How can one ever begin to think about a gift of Divine Life? I no longer call you servant but friend, son, brother, beloved. *Quid retribuam Domino pro omnibus quae retribuit mihi?*

*

A great full moon! No wonder men have adored it! Lord, didn't you know when you made it with all its enticing beauty that it would lead us astray? We have committed our own particular technological form of idolatry, spending millions and millions to set foot on it while our brothers and sisters here on earth starved to death—the human sacrifice offered on the altar of our ambitions.

*

When I see particular community needs, let me more often make prayer my response rather than action, at least in the first instance.

*

A superior must give first place to the calls of his office, setting them before the delights of contemplation in which he finds such happiness; and you, in your turn, my sons, must give first place to the peace and harmony of the community in which you live, preferring that to the great pleasure you have in prayer and contemplation. And lastly, my advice is this: never rely on your own opinion or judgment, but always seek advice and guidance of wiser members of your community in discerning the various changes and stages in your spiritual journey, whether it be that you are going down to Nazareth or up to the temple of Jerusalem.

———Aelred of Rievaulx

*

Really seek Jesus in the gospels and epistles each day.

*   *   *

The Abbot has asked us to answer four questions:
1. What is the most important monastic value for you?
2. What is the most important monastic value of our community for the Church and society?
3. What are the most important issues in our community today?
4. How is the community facing these?

The answers to questions 1 and 2 are obviously "love." Is our monastic life truly a School of Love, true love, the Love who is the Holy Spirit and our participation in that Love? Is it lived in such wise that Church and society not only receive it but can experience it? Is there effective witness to what is central in all life?

Issues: Fraternal and social love and contemplative freedom, simplicity of life in an affluent environment, identity with the poor, self-support and a contemplative pace of life, pluralism and incarnated unity.

How is the community facing these?

Judging by the good feedback from outsiders, well; from the Abbot General: needs are mounting and becoming crucial; in my own estimation: both are true.

Saint Clare

Saint Clare was canonized forty years after she entered the convent (1215–55), and yet we boast of having spent forty-six years in religious life—and we are still far from sanctity. Why are we wasting time? It doesn't take years or even minutes to become a saint. It only takes that fraction of a moment needed to turn wholly to the Lord—to say in fact, not words: My God and my *All.*

But, in fact, we cannot do it. Only he can accomplish it in us by his Holy Spirit. We do not know how to pray as we ought, but the Holy Spirit prays within us. Come, Holy Spirit. Pray for us, Saint Clare.

*   *   *

It continues to rain heavily. "He pours down generous rains."

——Psalm 67

*

Like Naaman, the Syrian, we tend to have our own ideas about how God should go about healing us. But God uses the ordinary everyday things and events—and we miss what is going on.

*

Brother Richard makes wonderful bread—many different kinds: whole wheat, rye, raisin-nut, dark brown—loaves that are round, large and small, long and short. But I am sure what makes it so good is the love he kneads into it all. Rich and I were novices together, and it seems to me he has been in the kitchen most of these thirty years, always teaching novices, but staying on himself. And always open to trying new things. Yesterday it was Chinese shrimp rolls.

The Assumption, Our Patronal Feast

Father Matthew gave a beautiful sermon this morning on the reciprocal munificence of God and the monk. Saturday I took a retreat day and tramped in the woods. Yesterday was retreat Sunday and I spent several hours before our Lord. Then I got called away to hear a confession just as we were to begin First Vespers of the Feast.

*

During the past month I have been resolving some problems.

The eremitical vocation is probably not for me. I will give it no more serious thought. It largely grew out of a false understanding of its place in the Cistercian way. I am convinced I am called to be a Cistercian and to find God in the Cistercian way. In the Cistercian way, I then seemed to see a built-in conflict between seeking God alone and real community life. Saturday, I saw the answer to this. To love and serve the brethren in true charity cannot interfere with seeking God alone—because God is love and the brethren are one in him, one with him. "Whatever you do to the least. . . ." The conflict I have experienced comes from the conflict between self-love (seeking self, self-gratification, in my love and service of others) and true charity. My painful prayer now is that I may love and serve purely and humbly and die to self and ambition, which has been so strong in me.

*

Practical resolves:
>   One hour of mental prayer over the required,
>   usually after Vigils.
>   One hour of really serious theological study,
>   usually the first hour of the work period.
>   Preparation for the Office from the first bell.

A couple of the brethren who need help to integrate into the community are coming to me—to help them and others and to help get my own house in order: more fasting—only water to drink at dinner and supper—no dessert—less at mixt.

*

It was a joy to see on the high altar some of the dahlias I had planted.

I ended up celebrating three Masses today: the early Mass for the Brothers, the High Mass, and a Mass at eleven for Sister Gabriel and the Sisters from Lowell. After Mass we had a picnic by the lake.

Saint Guerric's Day

May he bless us all with the spirit he received from Saint Bernard.

*

A bit of a headache. Feeling a bit pressed. Yesterday was a day of unending meetings, interviews, hospitality.

*

Lord, so near yet so far. Which is true? Or are both? You seem to be a constant most intimate companion to whom I can turn at any moment. And yet I find such alien desires grasping at my heart that I wonder if you are not far from me. But that is not you. You are all mercy and love and fidelity. Yes. But you are justice, too.

Saint Bernard's Day

The abbot goes to Wrentham today for the election of the abbess.

I am feeling a bit restless—perhaps because I have so much to do, so that even though I am moving quietly along, it is lodged in the background. I think I will be able to handle the classes well enough, although Saint Bernard is really too much. We will try simply to meet him and get in touch with his relation to Saint Benedict. That is about all we can hope to do this year.

Too many plans, too many things going. Not enough empty spaces. Lord, have mercy.

*   *   *

Doctor Hilary gave us some good points on freedom and community:

There are four kinds of freedom:

- *Ego* freedom—the freedom claimed to do whatever one's feelings or desires dictate. The true person here is more truly the slave—slave of his own passion.
- Then there is *conditioned* freedom, when one begins to accept himself as a social person and restricts himself by the rights of others.
- *Disciplined* freedom comes when one begins to get in touch with true values, the aspirations of his true self, and makes these the norms of his activity, curbing his own passions.
- Finally, there is *unconditional* freedom, when the integrated person can be wholly open to reality, completely vulnerable yet untouchable because he is wholly free to be.

*   *   *

Lord, something deep within me cries out to you, it thirsts for you. In spite of all the activities, all the people who have a claim on my time, in spite of the weariness that often makes prayer difficult and sleep appealing, in spite of the desires to read and write—the crying is there and continually surfaces. Lord, I thirst for you. I sit in the back of the church and my inners all stretch out to the tabernacle and draw water, living water from the fountain of your heart, the true source, the unfailing source, my source. Lord, come to me over the waters. Console my aching longing.

Feast of the Immaculate Heart of Mary

I went down to the garden as soon as it was light to get some flowers for Mary's shrine.

The discussion last night was disappointing. Instead of a real discussion among the brethren, the Abbot turned it into a feedback session for himself, and spent most of the time elaborating his own teaching. In itself that wasn't bad—in fact it was quite rich—but it was not what we expected.

I have so many things buzzing around in my head right now, with all the candidates' activities and the trip. Although I am constantly communing with our Lord, it is difficult to sense space, peace, contemplative freedom.

On the whole, though, it has been a day that unfolded rich in life, love and beauty, in ways not planned or expected.

John is here, seeing the vocation board. He is a gawky kid, about thirty, but good, good. I think he will make a good monk—open and receptive.

Pat arrived, an hour and a half late. He is balding, pot-bellied, an aging twenty-five. He didn't look too promising, but as we shared and he opened out more and more, telling things he had never told anyone before, I found a very loving, sensitive, good person, somewhat insecure, who let himself go and followed a phlegmatic temperament when the need for him at home and a love affair both ended and life had no great meaning. With a little encouragement, the Spirit will get him going again . . .

In the afternoon I shared with a prayer group at Mary House. What beautiful persons! We experienced a call to fuller transcendence and living in relation to it.

I ate too much at supper, especially the chocolate chip cookies. I have to get on top of that!

Watching the sunset, sitting at the church door, a cool, clear evening, becoming breezy. A not particularly spectacular slipping of the sun behind the horizon clouds. But really—the wonder of it all. Even the drooning plane and the soaring birds. The succession of day and night, of waking and sleeping . . .

*   *   *

Doctor Hilary gave us another talk: What monks have to teach the world. From a sociological point of view—his field— he thought they give an example of a community without family ties, having an affective relationship that is consequent upon organization. They exemplify disciplined freedom and social integration, that love and conflict are not opposites, and that there are many forms love can take. From a spiritual point of view, he sees monks as demonstrating the importance of prayer, solitude, and sacred space.

*   *   *

A man will wash his hands more for guests than for his own family.

——Chinese proverb

*   *   *

It is strange. With all the traveling I have done, as a trip approaches I can still sense a certain apprehension growing in me. Maybe it is the sense that "it is not expedient for a monk to be outside his enclosure." We are exotic plants that are oddities outside. It is hard for us to be true to ourselves and our way when in the busy worldly climate, with all its superficial and distracting demands. People leave little time and space for real meetings, for the Lord, for even the true self. Life in the cloister is geared to silence, coming to self, experiencing God, others, creation, more integrally touching mystery—being to and with.

*   *   *

The human adventure of marriage is tremendous, yet it is not enough for the human heart. God made marriage a sacrament, opening out upon the Infinite, and that alone can satisfy the human heart.

*   *   *

Robert challenged the community's lethargy at the opening of the Liturgy today. Perhaps he was a bit pessimistic, giving vent to some of his frustrations. For a man who knows liturgy so profoundly and is nationally respected for his work, he finds very little response in his own community: A prophet is not without honor except in his own country and among his own people. I am told a couple of the brethren were not happy ... I felt regret that there is so little tolerance, not to speak of loving compassion in our responses, at times. There was a summit meeting after Vespers—even though the Abbot is unwell—and Robert put up a note of apology, for which I greatly admire him. I don't know if I would have done the same.

*   *   *

Can he also give us bread to eat in the wilderness?
——Psalm 77

The Lord worked all sorts of wonders for his people and gave them manna from heaven and water from the rock, yet they questioned his ability to provide for their needs. We are like them. He has given us life, grace, sacraments, years and and years of loving care and sustenance, and yet we question if he will give the particular need of the moment, instead of just looking to him with confidence.

*   *   *

We are in the midst of a great lightning storm and rain—heavy rain. At one moment it seemed as though the lightning had struck the church itself. The Lord puts on brilliant spectacles. We have been getting a lot of rain of late. I can recall other—another close strike—Augusts, when we prayed long and hard for this. Another close strike!

* * *

Another month gone! It's hard to believe it! Certainly the contemplative life is not boring. My contemplative life, I am afraid, is also very active. Is there anything I can do to slow down? I don't see anything at the moment. All that I am doing seems to be a part of the obedience given me. I should certainly be watchful not to add anything further to activate it.

Thank God for the great silence and the long morning prayer!

* * *

Today I started a course on Saint Bernard. I feel great diffidence in trying to present such a great, almost giant person. I have been praying over it a lot. I trust the Lord will accomplish through it what he wants to accomplish. I sense the presence and closeness of Saint Bernard and rely on it. He himself will teach the minds and hearts of his sons. The same charism that was alive in Bernard is alive in us, so we have a sort of connatural affinity with him; his writings should resonate in our hearts. We seek, not primarily knowledge, but wisdom, savor, a mystical sensing of the Mystery as he sensed him who is the Beloved.

Who is this Jesus Christ? What does it mean when I say he is the Bridegroom of my soul? Am I comfortable with such imagery? How do I take it? It is certainly the imagery of God himself. And I think it can be taken with great concreteness. God, if anyone ever was, is earthy in his relation with his creature man. He took earth and formed him. He gave him the earth to play with, to work with, to suffer with, because of his sin. It is all sacrament—sign and symbol—of his love. Like the bride, man is to lay himself open with longing love to be penetrated by the thrusts of Divine Passion and then to embrace the Divine Lover and be wholly one with him, every part of his being impregnated with and resonating to the Divine Life that is being infused into and shared with him so that his own life might be divine, and with God, his lover, be fruitful and creative of life. As Saint Bernard so often says, only experience can begin to teach us the meaning of all this.

Come, Divine Lover!

*   *   *

Monthly Retreat Day

We have decided to observe complete silence on the monthly retreat day. I asked the candidates to do the same, so I had a very free day with the Lord. I overslept by accident, but am grateful for the extra rest. In the morning I finally got caught up on the mail. Then I spent the afternoon with the Lord as the Blessed Sacrament was exposed. It was good time. I see some of the areas where I have been cutting corners on the Lord and I resolve to do better. In three weeks I will be starting my solitary retreat. I should begin praying for that.

I feel quite happy and content. I should do more reading and reflecting to intensify my desire for Jesus and for heaven.

*

I do keep busy. Do I really want Mary's part? In the early morning hours I need to be watchful lest I fall asleep. Later in the day I need to make more time and gracious space and get time with the Lord in the Gospels.

*   *   *

Whenever he slaughtered them they sought him, they came to their senses and sought him earnestly, remembering that God was their rock, God the Most High their redeemer.
——Psalm 78:24–25

How true this is of us! When things are going fine, we so often are not true to God in our hearts, unfaithful to our baptismal covenant. But when the hand of the Lord is upon us, or affliction comes our way, we fall to our prayers in earnest and begin to pray without ceasing. In this sense, like Saint Paul, we can glory in our infirmities, because they do stimulate us to be more faithful to who we really are and to be more conscious of our real relation with God, our complete and total dependence. If through deep prayer we can learn to live in the reality, in the context of complete dependence and constant response to Presence, we will find that the fruits of the Spirit— love, joy, peace—prevail in our lives and our afflictions are relatively few and do not touch that deep inner sanctuary where these fruits are enjoyed. There we experience the wonder of how much we are truly loved and constantly held in caring love.

*   *   *

In the reading at Vigils, Archbishop Bloom spoke of devotion which must push one beyond spontaneity. Spontaneity, if it means going with the feelings, can be no more than animal. But true spontaneity, that which comes from our free will, is truly human. Devotion—*de vovere*—is from the will. It goes on, no matter how we feel; it goes beyond what we feel.

We can get narcissistic in our meditation. The community with its great demands is the safeguard against this. "If a man be alone, whose feet will he wash?" All traditions seek to keep the disciple from getting settled in his own meditation. In Zen you just get settled on your cushion and "gong," and you are off walking or running. Then you go to see the master and he shouts at you and hits you with his little stick and calls you names. In integral Yoga there is bhakti and karma to complement jana and hatha. In our life there are the brethren, office, and work—the primal cure that God gave Adam: "By the sweat of your brow. . . ." At first, in meditation, we leave all behind and we are in danger of centering on self. But when we truly seek God and find him, we find all in him and all the cares and pains of the aching world become ours. Rare indeed is the call to a purely eremitical life, but even there there is almost always some work, a communion with creation with its frustrating demands. Just try chopping some wood or keeping a cell clean with regular fidelity—how little things can magnify in the silent aloneness. And there is the cardinal law of the hermit's way: open and generous hospitality. The Lord will see that his servant is "pestered" by enough demands to ward off a threatening narcissism.

*

Courage and a man's part, that is what I ask of you; no room for fear and shrinking back, when the Lord your God is at your side wherever you go.

——Joshua 1:9

*

Hurricane David has wiped our skies very clear. There is not the least speck of haze in all the vast expanse. A great full moon gives light to all the night scene. A brisk refreshing breeze clasps the trees and lifts up spirits. A hurricane that brought terror and havoc to so many—over one thousand dead—has brought only refreshment and beauty to us. How mysterious are the ways of the Lord!

*   *   *

A disappointing note from _____. He finds regular celebration of the Sacrament of Reconciliation "too taxing" so he is going to discontinue. When monks let go of the values of their lives instead of creatively responding to the challenge of acedia, there is little hope for a full vibrant love-life in the Lord. That is true of any life. Making love to one's wife is bound to begin to appear at times as routine, of obligation, taxing. But if one stops, the marriage may well die. If one sees it as a challenge and seeks to respond to it creatively, the marriage can find new life. The same holds for any relation, any life, any human endeavor.

*   *   *

During the past two months a deepening brotherly friendship has been growing and is being fully experienced and enjoyed. As once before, such an experience is giving me deeper realization as to the kind of loving friendship Jesus, especially in the Eucharist, is looking for with me. I realize more the very deep hurt his love experienced in Judas and all us lesser Judases. I realize more the meaning of lovingly taking the Eucharist into my hands and my body. It is the embrace of a loving friend, a living person, a true expression of human and divine love in a total human way, involving body and soul.

*

In every true friend you have the greatest enemy to what is lowest in yourself.

*

When another comes to us in his loneliness, the quick comforting word is not the first or best response. First let us respond to the real loneliness that is there by sharing it. In the deep emptiness and nothingness we need to experience the potential and the hope. Not curing but caring.

*

We bring the Word to others so that we can hear back the Word.

*

Friendship is the most potentially dangerous of all affections.

——Aelred of Rievaulx

*

Signs of true spiritual friendship:
- It aids in the practice of virtue and the duties of one's state of life.
- It does not interfere with prayer.
- It seeks the genuine good of the friend.
- It does not tend to improper physical manifestations.

- It does not seek recompense for the good done to the friend.
- It will prudently correct *some* defects in the friend and put up with others.
- It is unwavering—not shaken by defects.
- Love of God grows with it—thoughts of the friend increase desire for God.

Signs of pseudo-spiritual friendship:
- It absorbs thought and attention, leaving one restless in the absence of the friend.
- It tends to be exclusive.
- It gives rise to jealousy and dislike for others.
- It leads to excess.
- A disproportionate time is spent with the "friend" in useless conversations.
- Love of God becomes cooler.
- There is an inordinate hiding of the friend's faults or over-readiness to expose them.
- There is frequent exchange of small gifts.

*   *   *

I have done poorly on the practical resolves of last month: falling asleep at the extra hour of prayer, missing the hour of study—though often not through my fault—not consciously preparing for the office from the first bell with regularity, doing little on fasting, taking beer whenever it is served, and eating the dessert—the fresh fruits from our orchards. I will try to do better on all these points.

*   *   *

I spoke to the candidates last night for forty-five minutes, just sort of rambling on. I prefer dialogue—interplay, but sometimes they just sit there, waiting to be fed. Maybe the fault is mine—I don't know how to evoke active response. Or maybe it is good for them to be fed. I lack confidence in the value of what I have to say—not the value of the content, for it is a poor expression of the most sublime—but the value of my saying it in the way I say it, even though the feedback is invariably positive. But I feel the negative isn't expressed, if it is there. The brethren are slow to express the negative—how much more the candidates, who too often feel they have to win me over. Lord, please use me for them, and you and your joy in them. *Miserere mei peccatore.*

The Nativity of Our Lady

The anniversary of my solemn vows. Thank you, Lord.

Four of us made vows and were consecrated that day at the Pontifical Mass. Jack got dispensed and is now gone from the earth, murdered by a demented person. John is wandering, seeking some ideal monastic home. Frank is superior of Genesee's foundation in Brazil. And I am still here at Spencer, by God's most gratuitous grace—the one of the four least worthy and least likely. But what is the quality of my being here? Lord, have mercy. I am still full of self-will, pride, stubborness and attachments of every sort. But also, I belong to Mary and this is her house.

*

The gladiolas from my garden are before the altar, just a big bunch, looking better than if they had been carefully arranged. They have their own beauty.

*   *   *

A fresh fall morning,
    A sunrise,
Diamonds of dew, lacing the
    petals of the red roses,
    A buzzing bee . . .
The monastery bell shatters
    the still air,
God is in his heaven,
    man is ready for another day of life.
May it be a day of hope,
    true life, love.

*

My poor mind is constantly on the go—often with the minutiae of my doings. I need to take a more resolute stand on quieting the interior dialogue. Especially do I need to watch out for resentful feelings and letting them sap strength and undermine a joy-full response to the candidates and the brethren. I think a lot of my tiredness comes from unnecessary thinking and not resting enough in the simple present and Presence.

*   *   *

A quiet day, cool and brisk. Only one candidate in the cottage. We celebrated the Byzantine Liturgy this morning. Then I picked the Easter lilies that had bloomed again, trumpeting the Easter joy again in their sweet odor.

*

We had a good movie last night on Judaism. A Pharisee explained how the Sabbath restrictions gave freedom for enjoyment. A professor who had lived through the internment camps and lost all his family in the holocaust pointed out: all the victims were Jews, all the killers were Christians. What is our response to that? I thought of Edith Stein and the Loeb family—Jews, yes, but also Christians. For the rest, we can only humble ourselves before the Lord.

*   *   *

Will Wil be coming today? It will be strange meeting him after so many years. A long letter from Jim this week—another college mate—how the past catches up with us! It is all with us, in us, in our core being, in who we are in the eternal being we are in God. Each one who enters our hearts is there forever. Each time we go before the Lord in prayer, he sees all our loves and blesses them. At length the day will come when we can indeed enjoy each other without ceasing in our Father's house.

There are many dwelling places in my Father's house;
otherwise how could I have said to you, I am going
away to prepare a home for you? And though I do go
away, to prepare you a home, I am coming back; and
then I will take you to myself, so that you too may be
where I am. . . . He who believes in the Son possesses
eternal life, whereas he who refuses to believe in the
Son will never see life.

——John 14:2; 3:35

*   *   *

Last night there was a sharing on the Retreat Day Silence.
It isn't that significant for me. Why? Partly because I have
usually spent retreat days much in silence, before the Sacrament. But also there is the question of interior silence. I
generally need to attend more to that. I have too many things
wheeling in my mind most of the time. I always have quite a
few projects going: with the candidates, writing, and other
things I get into. My life is not simple. I need to clean house, to
get rid of all unnecessary projects. More important, I need to
so focus all on the Lord that each leading points directly to
him. There is a simplicity of lack—nothing there. We can't get
too far with that unless we are unfortunate morons. And there
is a simplicity of fullness—like God's—an image of his—totally
simple but containing all—simple because all is ordered wholly
and seen wholly in its ordination as an expression of the one
divine reality of God's creative love, which is himself. I need to
keep life uncluttered because I have the grace to handle only
what he wants me to handle. With his grace, all of that can be
brought into the single current of responsive love and thus
never be divisive or dissipating, but rather expressive of and
intensifying that love.

Feast of the Most Holy Cross

During the morning meditation I heard the siren of the
Spencer Rescue Squad coming in our direction. It seemed to
stop quite close. Who? One of our neighbors? One of our own?

I held them all in my heart before the Lord in silence. We know not the day nor the hour. Yesterday we heard that Father Ted's tumor is malignant and then we heard that the new young novice master at Gethsemani was hospitalized with cancer.

I wonder just how I will respond if ever I receive such a verdict. At this theoretical distance I can say: With joy! Life is a journey, a pilgrimage, a going to our true home. News that the journey is near its end, the goal is in sight, would be good news. Yet my Master sweat blood in Gethsemani. Was it because of the type of death, or the burden of sin he took on, or because he really understood, fully experienced, the horror of death—the always violent wrenching apart of what is one whole—the precious reality of a human person?

Feast of the Seven Sorrows of Our Blessed Mother

I have quite a headache this morning. I slept fitfully last night—unusual for me. I am not sure why. Before turning out the light I read a bit of Bill Kienzle's *Rosary Murders.* During Vigils I was distracted by the idea of writing a monastic whodunit (maybe getting some vicarious satisfaction in killing off some of the brethren). Maybe this was percolating through my mind during the night. A curious thing—I rarely remember my dreams, but most of the dreams that I have remembered in the past year have been murder mysteries. I think I could enjoy writing one. But for the moment I think I'll put it aside—I'm too busy, but also I need time for discernment on it.

*

Today's feast is special and I have a big bouquet of flowers before the altar. (My! All I did was plant some bulbs, do a little weeding, and cut them. How quickly we take credit and get possessive!) I am going to lie down and meditate on Mary's sorrows after I finish my nut bread and coffee.

*   *   *

I have the early Mass this week.

Things are winding down. It will be a busy day, but one candidate leaves, tomorrow two more, then only one remains. Classes are finished. Correspondence is caught up for the most part. So I move toward my retreat with eager anticipation. May it be a real time of rendezvous with the Lord—a time of conversion and renewal.

*   *   *

Ted just left—a warm, loving, gentle person. May the Lord give him the grace of this holy vocation.

*   *   *

I feel a great need of prayer. What is prayer? A kind of longing hunger for God. Who is God? Some—I almost said "... body," but that is part of it. He is not "body" except in Jesus—a body long ascended, now only mystically experienced, especially in the Eucharist. I hesitate even to say "someone"—one seems too narrowing, material. I know him, yet I don't. He is all, yet he is passionately particular and responsive and loving. He is mystery, as is any loved person, yet more so. I am totally drawn to him when I am at home, most truly with myself, when I do not let the fascination of trifles—all are trifles compared to him, yet in themselves almost infinitely precious, if not truly infinitely precious, when they are his own beloved images—obscure the good. I sit dumbly, stupidly, longingly, lovingly, painfully, hurting, before him. Lord, be merciful to me, your sinner. I am not worthy yet I desperately need—need you.

*   *   *

I stayed up too late last night, reading. I read a very challenging dialogue on abortion between Lucien Miller, a professor of Amherst, Father Mark, our doctor, a rabbi, and a minister. The minister worked from situation ethics, argued for complete non-violence, but saw everyone failing and felt abortion was the least sort of failure—a phenomenological approach that values things according to his own experience of them. The rabbi proclaimed the great reverence for life of his tradition, yet did abortion referral. When it comes down to the line, how few of us are consistent with our values in an integral way!

*

A servant of the Lord has no business with quarreling; he must be kindly towards all men, persuasive and tolerant, with a gentle hand for correcting those who are obstinate in their errors. It may be that God will enable them to repent and acknowledge the truth, so they will recover their senses and shake off the snare by which the devil, till now, has held them prisoners to his will.

——2 Timothy 2:24ff

*   *   *

Ideas for books are frequently running around in my head. What to do with them? On the one hand I am happy for them—I don't want to lose them. On the other, I don't want even this kind of "productivity" to be taking me from deeper prayer. I should practice what I preach about centering and let them go until it is time to work with them.

*   *   *

All ready to leave for my long-awaited retreat. All ready, as usual, well in advance of departure time, and feeling a bit nervous as I always do when leaving the abbey and embarking on a trip. The day is crystal-clear, so there should be no difficulty with flights. May the Lord watch over all my ways and may my coming bring him more into each life I touch. I am dressed in clericals—unusual for me, though I suspect it will become more usual. As I get older I get more conservative and conforming—though I do feel uncomfortable in the collar. It is difficult to decide what is the most appropriate attire for a monk outside of his monastery: a modified habit like the one Brother David Steindl-Rast wears, clericals, a cross, or just secular attire? I have done all over the years. The time, place, and occasion have their demands.

Already I feel it will be good to get back home.

IN RETREAT

In Retreat

Here I am, at Mercy at last! Mercy, the place to be, deep in God's Mercy. I can hear the waves outside my window, crashing on the shore. The Blessed Sacrament is a few yards away on the sun porch. I have a large room with a large window on the sea.

Here I am at last, at the beginning of this long-awaited retreat. May Mercy have his way with me! Mercy will be the theme of this retreat. Living in God's mercy—what joy, what peace, what confidence, what hope! Mercy—how much I need to be like God in his mercy. "Blessed are the merciful for they shall obtain mercy." During these days, may I come to know God's mercy more fully and learn better how to be merciful myself.

*

Judges 21: The Israelites, after they defeated and severely punished the Benjaminites, mourned the loss of their brothers and did all they could to restore them—such is mercy.

*

In heaven we shall have the insight to see that the particular reward or beatitude that is ours is the most perfect possible good for us.

*   *   *

I am sitting on the sand, watching, listening to the waves as the evening tide brings them closer. I thank you, God, for the wonder of my being—for my being. It is difficult for us to grasp the full significance of this gift. A gift is usually given to someone, but in this case the someone did not yet exist. The gift was the someone. This is mercy.

163

*

It is difficult to conceive of the world without "me." Because, in fact, I tend to conceive of the world with "me" at the center, everything revolving around me. The whole project seems to lose its meaning, as far as I am concerned, when I am no longer at the center. When I step back from this egocentric position and picture such a world, there seems to be a real hole in it without "me." And this is not wholly foreign to the truth of the reality. As God has planned things, as the world has existed in his love through all eternity, I am part of it. Without me, this world would be incomplete; all creation is a gift to me. And I myself am gift to me. All is gift. All praise to the Giver!

What would this rambling mean to one who experiences life—his life—as miserable: a handicapped person, a man trapped in the slums, or a man enslaved to the bottle, a father who cannot provide a decent life for his family? The reality would not change. Life is still a wondrous gift. But man's sacrilegious abuse of it is blatant, sometimes more so than at other times. No man, woman or child should be denied reverence or a worthy share of the gifts of the creating Lord. May God have mercy on us for the way we serve his blessed creation.

*

Have you not seen him in the things he has made?

*

See as a child sees.

*

He who has a *why* to live can bear with almost any *how*.

——Nietzsche

*   *   *

When we witness from the Absolute, the true Self, the passing thoughts and feelings of the relative self, we can be detached, more fully appreciative. We can use them or let them go, and be fully present and not be captivated by these passing things. I need to center more, especially during this time of retreat, and practice stepping back from the relative passing things.

*

Discernment of desires and feelings:

Unworthy feelings and desires:
- They are unreasonable (unattainable or not pertinent to one's state in life); there is no proportion between the feelings and their cause.
- They leave the soul agitated and disturbed.
- They are ego-centric—directed to the self.
- They rest in the object of the desire for itself.
- They tend to be contrary to docility and obedience.
- They inspire self-exaltation and vanity.
- They tend toward sensuality, comfort, ease.
- They flow from the "common sense" of the world—a moderation that is mediocrity.

Worthy feelings and desires:
- They are reasonable (truly attainable) and proportionate to their causes.
- They leave true peace.
- They are directed toward God, his glory, and the good of souls.
- They do not cling to the object for itself.
- They tend to remain in the framework of obedience.
- They inspire humility and subjection.
- They tend to imitate Christ, and involve self-denial and mortification.
- They are based on and grow out of a strong spirit of faith and supernatural prudence.

*   *   *

Discretion is blinded by two things: anger and extreme softheartedness.

—Saint Bernard

*   *   *

I have been reading Saint Aelred's *Mirror of Charity,* the primer of Cistercian life. He makes it clear that the burdensome yoke is not Christ's but that of our own possessions and possessiveness. How true! Lord, free me in your great mercy.

*

There will be greater happiness for those whose capacity is less, if they can make their own what is possessed by others whose capacity is greater. . . . We do this when we both love them and the goodness in them.

*

We must seek to enjoy one another in God, and at the same time to enjoy God in each other.

*

How can one lay down any general rule when there are so many different sorts of men to consider, so many different qualities involved in considering each individual?. . . so each one of you must use his own common sense and apply the rule according to his needs.

*

The things which God allows us in this life are all pure to the pure, and none of them is to be rejected. All are to be accepted with gratitude.

*

Too much concentration on one fault may blind us to the fact that we have others which also need to be dealt with.

——Saint Aelred

*

Whatever we think necessary to do for our own salvation, can be equally necessary for the salvation of others.

*   *   *

Where is this retreat going? I don't know. Should I know? Should I be spending more time in formal prayer? What kind of formal prayer? I am before God in God and ache for more. More what? Presence? Understanding? Being? What is, is. And only God can make me to be more. Can I merit it? Isn't it all mercy? I am in Mercy. What more is there? Thy will be done.

Do I really want only that: His will be done in me, in all, in all things? Yes, Lord. Help my hesitations. I seek to be free to but rest in him. But when I get the time for such rest, I begin to be restless. Something in me urges: I must do. No! I must be. And do only when he wants, how he wants. Amen, Lord. So be it. Help my stupid prideful restlessness.

*

He who still knows how intensely he is praying has not overcome the bonds of self.

——Or Ha-Emet

*

Ba'al Shem Tov's thought was most revolutionary. Just as in life he taught that each moment may be an opening to the Presence of God, so in prayer he taught that each distraction may become a ladder by which one may ascend to a new level of devotion. For if one truly believes that all things are from God and bear his mark, he can make no exception for the fantasies of his own mind! They too are from God and are sent to us as ways to his service. The worshipper must break open the shell of evil surrounding the distracting thought, find the root of that thought in God, and join it to his prayer.

——Arthur Green

*

The words of prayer fly upward and come before God. As God turns to look at the ascending word, life flows through all the worlds and prayer receives its answer.

——Or Torah

*

Do not think that the words of prayer as you say them go up to God. It is not the words themselves that ascend; it is rather the burning desire of your heart that rises like smoke toward heaven.

——Or Ha-Me'ir

*

I understand that prayer (and those lives given to it) is the energy by which God unites the world to himself.

——Marilyn Bendzwill

*   *   *

We need to really give ourselves—all that we are, all that we have—to the Lord, holding nothing back. It is like the loaves and fishes—all they had was five loaves—barley, at that, the bread of the poor—and two fishes—and these they had received from others. Yet they gave all into the hands of the Lord. And when he had finished using them and accomplishing great things through them, they found themselves with basketfuls. When the Lord uses us for others, in the end we get the most out of it. That is his most loving way. But unless the grain of wheat does fall into the ground and die—let go of everything—it remains itself alone.

*

At Communion again today I heard the song: *Take, Lord, receive.* I had heard it earlier in the week. It is becoming part of my retreat, its theme:

Take, Lord, receive all my liberty, my memory,
     my understanding, my entire will.
Give me only your love and your grace:
     that's enough for me.
     Your love and your grace are enough for me.
Take, Lord, receive all I have and possess.
     You have given all to me;
     now I return it.
Give me only your love and your grace:
     that's enough for me.
     Your love and your grace are enough for me.
Take, Lord, receive, all is yours now;
     dispose of it wholly according to your will.
Give me only your love and your grace:
     that's enough for me.
     Your love and your grace are enough for me.

*

" . . . on waking, I shall be content in your presence."
——Psalm 17:15

I have learned to sleep with the sunshine fully on my face.
——William of Saint Thierry

When we really wake up we will know that you are our God and our *all*—your love and your grace are enough. Lord, wake me up!

*

My reason's eyes are dazzled when I try to look at him. As best I can, I wipe the rheum of my long sleep from them with the hand of exercises.

——William of Saint Thierry

*

Though he fall, he does not lie prostrate, for the hand of the Lord sustains him.

——Psalm 37:24

*   *   *

Nothing particularly great or outstanding today. I slept late. Mass at 11:00. After lunch I walked and prayed. Another Mass at 3:30. I began reading Saint Bernard's *Steps of Humility.* Being, more than doing.

*

How, after the revelation of himself to himself, can a man lift up his eyes and walk with head erect?. . . the soul can find no motive more effective for humility than a knowledge of itself as it really is . . . and obtaining this knowledge, how can it be otherwise than humbled?

*

You will never have real mercy for the failings of others until you know and realize that you have the same failings in your own soul.

——Saint Bernard

*

We can receive God's mercy only when we admit our misery—our need for mercy.

* * *

Lord, in the simplicity of my heart I will gladly give you all.

*

The Lord loves a cheerful giver.
——2 Corinthians 9:7

*

I am your reward exceedingly great.
——Genesis 15:1

*

For what do I have in heaven, and what besides you do I want on earth, God of my heart and my portion forever?
——Psalm 72:25f

* * *

There is only one world, and it is the home of all.

*

Our task is like that of the builders of the pyramids in Mexico or Egypt, of the temples in Asia, of the stone carvers of the great cathedrals of Europe. We do not see the whole finished work, but we have our part in producing a thing of beauty that is to last forever. We have to have confidence in the vision we serve.

*

Everyone around me needs my support, my care, my love. This is what the Church is all about—to know Christ as a friend who cares for me and for the person next to me, so that my attitude toward this person will be that of Christ. When we wonder about the mystery of ourselves we need to look to Christ who gives the meaning of life. When we wonder about the meaning of life we need to look to Christ who is perfect humanity.

*

Let us rejoice, for he is the master of our lives. Joy is the keynote of the good news and the heart of the Gospels. We are an Easter people and "Alleluia" is our song.

> J —— Jesus first
> O —— Others second
> Y —— You third

*

Nothing reveals true misery so much as untrue joy.
——Saint Bernard

*　　*　　*

The Vicar of Christ has just reached our country. It is a time, a season of special grace. His greeting: that we would live up to our eminent mission of service to the world.

In his homily in Boston, the Holy Father gave a wonderful rousing call to follow Christ, using the incident of the rich young man. Pouring rain diminished the crowd, but it was estimated at 100/250,000 with 7,000 security people.

The President spoke later on Cuba and our position on it. The contrast: a call to love and happiness and a call to a position of threat and violent power. How much we need a conversion of heart!

*

Past achievements are not an acceptable substitute for present responsibilities.

*

Freedom that was gained must every day be confirmed by the rejection of all that wounds human rights.

*

Make peace the desire of your hearts, for if you love peace, you will love all humanity.

*

Keep Jesus in your heart—then you will recognize him in each human being.

——John Paul II

*   *   *

The first reading today spoke very directly to me: From the time the Lord led us out of the land of Egypt until the present day, we have been disobedient to the Lord our God, and only too ready to disregard his voice. . . . he led us forth to give us a land flowing with milk and honey. For we did not heed the voice of the Lord our God in all the words of the prophets whom he sent us, but each one of us went off after the devices of our own wicked hearts, served other gods and did evil in the sight of the Lord our God.

God led me forth to the monastery. It should have been a life full of grace and joy—the fruits of the Spirit—but so often I have followed my own heart, one burdened by original sin and the seven capital sins and my own past sins. I have sought myself and other false gods. Lord, have mercy. May this retreat be a time of truest conversion.

I then read Ephesians 4. What a program for community life:

Bear with one another charitably, in complete selflessness, gentleness and patience. Do all you can to preserve the unity of the Spirit by the peace that binds you together. There is one Body, one Spirit, just as you were all called into one and the same hope when you were called. There is one Lord, one faith, one baptism, and one God who is Father of all, over all, through all and within all. . . .

Each one of us has been given his own share of grace, given as Christ allotted it . . . to some his gift was that they should be apostles; to some, prophets; to some, evangelists; to some, pastors and teachers; so that the saints together make a unity in the work of service, building up the body of Christ. In this way we are all to come to unity in our faith and in our knowledge of the Son of God, until we become the perfect Man, fully mature with the fullness of Christ himself. Then we shall not be children any longer, or tossed one way and another and carried along by every wind of doctrine, at the mercy of all the tricks men play and their cleverness in practicing deceit. If we live by the truth and in love, we shall grow in all ways into Christ, who is the head, by whom the whole body is fitted and joined together, every joint adding its own strength, for each separate part to work according to its function. So the body grows until it has built itself up, in love. . . .

You must give up your old way of life; you must put aside your old self, which gets corrupted by following illusory desires. Your mind must be renewed by a spiritual revolution so that you can put on the new self that has been created in God's way, in the goodness and holiness of the truth.

So from now on, there must be no more lies: *You must speak the truth to one another,* since we are all parts of one another. *Even if you are angry, you must not sin:* never let the sun set on your anger, or else you will give the devil a foothold. Anyone who was a thief must stop stealing: he should try to find some useful manual work, and be able to do some good by helping others that are in need. Guard against foul talk; let your words be for the improvement of others, as occasion offers, and do good to your listeners. Otherwise you will only be grieving the holy Spirit of God who has marked you with his seal for you to be set free when the day comes. Never have grudges against others, or lose your temper, or raise your voice to anybody, or call each other names, or allow any sort of spitefulness. Be friends with one another, and kind, forgiving each other as readily as God forgave you in Christ.

—Ephesians 4:2–7; 11–13; 22–32.

*   *   *

The gulls are lined up on the solitary rock, like so many rowers letting their skiff glide through the choppy sea. The sun runs along the crests to greet me with its warmth. The breeze that stirs the waters, freshens the air and pats my cheek. I sit under a red pine and look out at empty horizons that are full of hope. Over there, beyond, is my new home—someday. Lord, grant it if you will. The gull glides, it wings, it is free, but it does not know it; it only lives it.

*

No hurry to end. There must be an end to hurry.

*   *   *

The Good News includes some hard words—for, those whom he loves he reproves.

*   *   *

Ending a Retreat
- Rest always at the center of Mercy
- Take, Lord, receive. Your love and your grace are enough for me
- Ephesians 4

- A greater social awareness in response to the call of Pope John Paul II

I don't feel like writing up a schedule. I will very much follow what I have been doing, adding a bit:
- Increase the number of daily prostrations
- Take time for the moon and the stars and sunrises
- Listen to the Lord's daily message in the readings of the day

*

Those who have a sure hope, guaranteed by the Spirit, that they will rise again, lay hold of what lies in the future as though it were already present.
——Saint Cyril of Alexandria

THY KINGDOM COME!

Toward the Kingship of Christ

The Feast of Saint Luke

Saint Luke, the Evangelist of social concern, of women, of prayer—truly a man for our times. I think his is my favorite Gospel in many ways, though in the end I veer toward John and the outpourings of the Sacred Heart at the Last Supper.

*

Saint Benedict says every line of Sacred Scripture, every word, is a rule of life. I find that very true in Ephesians, especially the verse about speaking: Say only what will edify— build up. A hard enough rule to live by, but one that would change the complexion of the community if we all really adhered to it.

*

The Abbess came from Wrentham today with three of the nuns celebrating their silver jubilee. They got a full tour of the monastery—even my cell!

*

It is also the silver jubilee of Father Eugene's ordination to the priesthood. We had a special afternoon Mass so that his family and friends could be with us. Because of his very limited eyesight, Father is never principal celebrant, so it was a special joy to see him celebrate today with his Oblate brother as his assistant.

*   *   *

Some addenda to my retreat resolutions:
- Fidelity to at least four hours of prayer and personal *lectio.*

- Prayer—on my knees if possible—whenever I enter or leave my cell.
- Daily exercise, yoga.
- No work on Sundays and holydays.
- Be decisive in control of thoughts and actions.
- Work at continuous conscious response to the presence of God.
- Seek to be more generous in accepting discomfort.

To live as a

man	think and will
Christian	with Christ
monk	wholly consecrated
priest	mediating, caring for all

Saint Hedwig and Saint Margaret Mary

It certainly was a great manifestation of the love of the Sacred Heart for his Church when on the feast of this Patroness of Poland he gave his Church a Polish Pope! Last year he was unknown to us—today he is known and loved, a man who seems very close.

*

Yesterday I received a letter from a Clarist who said my writings do not convey the love and warmth that is in my face. I need to reflect on that, and let my writing flow more naturally and directly from my heart to the reader whom I love.

"If you could relax and write as happy, loving and friendly as you look . . ."

*

You must put aside, then, every trace of ill-will, and deceitfulness, your affectations, the grudges you bore, and all slanderous talk. You are a child newborn, and all your craving must be for the soul's pure milk, that will nurture you unto salvation, once you have tasted, as you have surely tasted, the goodness of the Lord.

——1 Peter 2:1ff

*   *   *

Yesterday the Abbot and others went to see the Dalai Lama at Barre and brought back a movie of him. I was not too impressed. I am looking forward to meeting him personally next week to see if I do experience something deeper in his regard. After the tremendous impact Pope John Paul made on us, others have a lot to measure up to.

*   *   *

Retreat Sunday—a day of great silence.

This morning at Vigils we read from Zephaniah:

Therefore, expect me—it is Yahweh who speaks—on the day I stand up to make my accusation; for I am determined to gather the nations, to assemble the kingdoms, and to pour out my fury on you, the whole heat of my anger.

Yes, I will then give the peoples lips that are clean, so that all may invoke the name of Yahweh and serve him under the same yoke. From beyond the banks of the rivers of Ethiopia my suppliants will bring me offerings.

When that day comes you need feel no shame for all the misdeeds you have committed against me, for I will remove your proud boasters from your midst: and you will cease to strut on my holy mountain. In your midst I will leave a humble and lowly people, and

those who are left in Israel will seek refuge in the
name of Yahweh.

——Zephaniah 3:8–12

There will be no shame at the general judgment when
everything is laid bare because all there will be meek and
humble and therefore truly compassionate and understanding.
A humble person is patient even in the face of unjust injuries
because he is compassionate, knowing the unjust one is as he is
because of his weakness and blindness.

*

Saint Teresa points out that God rewards our service with
trials, misunderstanding, injustice, aridity. It is the best thing
he can do for us because it helps us grow in love. We should
serve God not as mercenaries or day laborers, wanting our pay
each day, but rather as grandees who serve the King freely.
His favor is enough.

*   *   *

In the second reading at Vigils today, Henri Daniel-Rops
spoke of his years of infidelity, trying to reconcile the unrecon-
cilable and the misery that came from it. How much of the
unhappiness of my life comes from the same attempt?

*   *   *

It is 5:30 A.M. and I feel very foggy-headed and tired at the
moment. What is the best thing to do now? I would like to
settle into prayer but I fear that might end up in sleep. Should
I sit sipping coffee while I pray? Should I do something that
would better stimulate me and pray later? Should I get some
more sleep? How our humanity weighs upon us sometimes!
I lift up my hands in the night.

*   *   *

The Spirit came upon Mary and she became fruitful. The Spirit came upon the Church at Pentecost and she became fruitful (three thousand baptisms that first day). If we are to be fruitful, our fruitfulness can only come about by the coming of the Spirit upon us.

*

In the good creation there is no opposition between male and female; the sexes are rather sacramental of God's life-giving love and the creation's mediating that love in fruitfulness. God is known personally through his election of his People—his bride, so unfaithful. His creation in its fruitful fidelity is Wisdom, the personified feminine. His unfaithful bride of the Old Covenant is replaced by his new bride, the Church. Each soul, a member of the Church and summing up her whole reality in this present time and place, is bride, to be fruitful in receiving God's love—his Spirit. Marriage is then a sacrament, symbolizing in its physicality this great reality of creation and re-creation, of covenant and salvation history. Hence the great dignity and importance and sacredness of marriage and the tragedy of marital infidelity or deliberate unfruitfulness.

The two shall become one flesh. By Christ's union with his Church we become one flesh with him, a reality we celebrate in the Eucharist.

*

One thing I note, among others, in the majority of the young men I meet today—a better integration of the feminine. This is not true of all, obviously, but of very many. Some would say it is a blurring of the sexes or weak sexual identity. It may be true that with the more integral development, the intensity of both is somewhat less than if all the energies had been concentrated in one. But I have often discerned in those who have developed in only one direction a defensiveness toward their feminine side that has led to a certain superficiality in their masculinity. When a man is open to the feminine in himself he is usually open to others and to reality in a less defensive way and there tends to be a deeper, freer person, more able to express and receive love and caring. All of this is very healthy and Christlike. Our Lord did not hesitate to use feminine imagery in regard to himself and to be tenderly intimate as well as strongly male in his relations with his friends. We find the same in our Cistercian Fathers. This is to be encouraged.

*

Christ gives us his Body in communion. No truly human love can be complete without including in some way the gift of the body. Unfortunately our culture has come to identify all tactility as being ordered to genitality and so has condemned men to a hands-off attitude unless they want to be taken to be gay, or, with women, looking for something more.

Happily the charismatics have been finding the freedom to be more integral in their loving response to each other, though not without suffering criticism or derision from others. Monks have always kept a certain freedom in this regard. They do not hesitate to embrace one another warmly when it is called for. When tactility is so restricted it puts a strain on men, especially celibates. They are condemned to be very unaffectionate, rather cold persons, as unfortunately all too many of our priests and religious are, or to go too far and become promiscuous. The goodness of human affections expressed physically as well as verbally needs to be reaffirmed.

*   *   *

My little gardenia plant is dying—and there is nothing I can do about it. I wanted to take good care of it. It was a beautiful, healthy little plant when it arrived a week or two ago. It even had some buds. But in my solicitude I fear I gave it too much water. I didn't mean to harm it—only to help and care for it. But nature is relentless in her laws. No matter how well-intentioned we be, if we violate the laws of nature, nature will take her toll. We can see that on so many levels in our world today. Technology sought the advancement of man, but has brought it about that his very existence is in peril from ecological disaster. Couples in good subjective conscience try to foster their mutual life through birth control and even abortion, and marriage is going to pieces. Only a total gift of self in openness can ground a stable marriage, a love that trusts in God, makes him part of the love, and is able to face sacrifice together.

* * *

Masturbation is a failure in the contemplative attitude. It is usually a functioning at a very gross or materialistic level. It fails to be present to the reality that a man's giving forth of his seed is not just a pleasurable stimulating experience, an experience of power, a release of tension, but it is a pouring forth of something of his very self, something that is most vital in him, so vital that it has the potential of communicating his very life with all its genetic particularity. To communicate something so intimately himself to another implies the greatest act of trust, something he will never do lightly if he properly esteems himself. To pour himself forth into the void as a pure waste involves a profound frustration which he will experience even if he does not cognitively or evaluatively perceive it. The contemplative attitude is fully present to the "now" and perceptive of the deeper and deepest levels of reality. It is in touch with the full significance of a man's giving forth his seed and of the divine creative energies at play with and in man as he does this. In this reality, masturbation is perceived as a sacrilegious frustration.

* * *

Saint Ignatius of Antioch

We heard again at Vigils Saint Ignatius' stirring prayer to be ground by lions' teeth to be the bread of Christ. I found myself waiting for it as I read the long lesson. It was at the very end. It is a great thing when the Lord gives a man to utter a sentence that will rest in the Christian heart for centuries. It is usually the fruit of a lifetime of fidelity.

*   *   *

Father Prior just learned he has a serious case of diabetes—it is affecting his eyesight. He needs our special support these days.

*

Dennis called. He will be here Saturday to enter. Also Peter. How good is the Lord who shares such wonderful young brothers with us! May all their hopes be realized—and more!

The North American Martyrs

When I hear how these holy martyrs suffered I am ashamed of my little tolerance for sufferings and my unwillingness to seek and embrace the cross. May they intercede for all of us to live the cross more fully and be more generous in embracing the daily cross.

*   *   *

Archbishop Gerrity, who is on retreat with us this week, spoke of the experience of the Church of Newark. On the dark side he sees priests still leaving, few vocations, aging personnel, a mounting divorce rate, longer adolescence, ethnic and racial tensions. On the side of hope—and he comes across as an essentially hopeful man—he sees more study and prayer among the priests, more lay participation, especially in the Liturgy, more spiritual concern among the youth. He has a diocesan program called "RENEW." It is a program for renewal through scriptural meditation in small groups. He is quite excited about it.

*   *   *

I feel very tired today, even though it is just a short time since my retreat. Perhaps it comes from a certain psychological pressure, for we are having great fall weather and all is going well. There is a sense of having much to do. The cottage program demands seven days a week, and it looks as if it will be virtually non-stop. I have articles, talks, and books to get on with, and classes. The garden and cottage have things to be done. Each day's mail would be sufficient for the day's work, reading all that comes in and answering what has to be answered. I need to live in the "now," peacefully doing what is to be done, and not letting the pressure build up.

* * *

Frank Sheed, still hale and hearty despite his many years and miles, gave us a witty talk on the Church "being in a state" today, because we are not sufficiently grateful for the gift of the Church and her teaching. This is evident to him in the general lack of concern on the part of Catholics for sharing the faith with others. This man, who has stood so many thousands of hours on public platforms, giving witness to the Catholic truth, certainly has the right, if anyone does, to make such a criticism. And I find it true. Even among religious and priests there is a hesitation, and more, to share the faith and so strengthen each other in the face of a world that constantly pushes upon us other values and value systems and mocks the values we know are to our happiness as human persons and are for the eternal happiness of us all. Would that there were more courageous and generous laymen like this happy old crusader to challenge us out of our shyness or lethargy and call us forth to joyfully share what we have received.

*

And now, brethren, all that rings true, all that commands reverence, and all that makes for right; all that is pure, all that is lovely, all that is gracious in the telling; virtue and merit, wherever virtue and merit are found—let this be the argument of your thoughts.
——Philippians 4:8

*   *   *

Up to a certain point our needs are more psychological than real. We become convinced we need so much food, sleep, etc., to be happy, well, etc. But if we can shake off such convictions, and experiment a bit, we find a greater freedom and flexibility. But we have to really let go of our prejudices or they will cause fatigue, headache, etc., if they are not gratified, even though we may actually be better off eating less, sleeping less, exercising more, etc. We are sometimes hard put to have an inner understanding and compassion for the man or woman who is slave to the bottle or drugs or lust, but find ourselves caught with our own needs, for coffee, tea, cigarettes, or the like. We don't realize that our humanity is equally truncated by these addictions, even if they are not taking the same immediately obvious physical toll.

*   *   *

"I'm no good." That is *not* poverty of spirit. It's a lie. "I am nothing." A lie! "*Of myself,* I am nothing—and worse than nothing. A minus—for I am a sinner—and sin is a lack of due goodness and being." This is the reality. And grasping it is true poverty of spirit. The first step of the AA program is: admitting that of myself I am a hopeless case. God has to get us all there—existentially there, not just verbally—whether it is by drink, drugs, sex, anger, or distractions in prayer. When I am there I have finally made it to the first step of truth, the first beatitude, the gateway to the kingdom.

God has given us everything—even his own Son, and a share in his own life and being. That is why we are truly great. Yet there is one thing God cannot give us and still be God, and that is his glory, the fact that he is the ultimate source of all goodness. Yet we are so prone to pat ourselves on the back, to put our own signature at the bottom of the painting. Until we know existentially that from us of ourselves comes nothing except that lack of due good we call sin, we will tend to try to make ourselves gods by taking credit for God's goodness and sharing. But once we grasp this absolutely basic reality, then he can do all things in and through us, for we will always ascribe all good to him.

* * *

Saturday of Our Lady

Because the whole faith of the Church one Saturday—called Holy Saturday—resided in the faith of one Woman, every Saturday in the mind of the Church belongs in a special way to her. Where is our own faith as we come to encounter the Risen Lord this Saturday? What faith do we have in Mary?

* * *

The test is, whether we keep his commandments; the man who claims knowledge of him without keeping his commandments is a liar; truth does not dwell in such a man as that.

———John 2:3

* * *

Sunday

A day of joy and gratitude as two more receive the holy habit.

* * *

Today we hear Bartimeus: Lord, that I may see!

That is the fundamental prayer. If I could really see God, my whole being would be drawn to him—a total "yes" to his creating goodness and absolute beauty. And I would see the consonance of all good, the stupidity and desecration of all evil. Yet, there is another need. We are free. And we can unfortunately be perverse. I yet need his help to respond to the light, embrace the "yes."

Lord, enlighten my mind, stimulate my sluggish will. Lord, that I may see—and, like Bartimeus, begin to follow.

*   *   *

I am struggling with a cold—will probably try to get some extra rest. The Prior spoke yesterday about trying to be at Vigils and returning to rest afterwards if necessary. All the novices are usually at Vigils, but the professed do not do so well. Some of the more outspoken of the novices speak of a "double standard." Granted, as one gets older, needs arise. Yet it is some of the ancients who are most faithful.

*

> Come, then, praise the Lord, all you that are the Lord's servants; you that wait on the Lord's house at midnight, lift up your hands towards the sanctuary and bless the Lord.
>
> ——Psalm 133:1f

All Saints' Day

A glorious fall day. I am busy replying to the seventeen new inquiries that arrived in today's mail. May all these young men become saints!

*   *   *

All Souls' Day

Procession through the cemetery—quiet, meaningful.

When will we wend our way there again? Who will be next? The cemetery is a restful place, quiet, a place of prevailing hope. One almost looks forward to resting there. My journey ahead could yet be long. Father Bernard was fifty years my senior. Now I am older than some of the candidates' fathers. In time I could be older than their grandfathers. We count the years, but that is not what matters. It is the moment in which we say unconditionally, "Yes."

Father Xavier of New Ringgold Priory died in his sleep yesterday—age fifty-five.

Our journey may be nearer the end than we think. To go to sleep and suddenly slip out of the body and be before our Lord Jesus . . . Wonderful!—yet how soiled we are! But will not the flood of the love of this our Friend immediately bathe us: Lord, I am not worthy—of you, of entering into the Kingdom—but only say the word, and I shall be cleansed, healed, covered with the garments of the First Born.

Saint Bernard, at the end of his treatise on *Precepts and Dispensation*, reminds us that the Kingdom of God is within. If we have each day made that journey within, our passing will be to no strange place. Only the limitation of faith, the veil that leaves God invisible, will be lifted or fall away, and we shall see him who has always been dwelling at the center of our being with his gift of being and life and all that is.

May the Lord, when he calls, even if it be as a thief in the night, find me ready because I have spent time regularly, almost constantly, within. And may our beloved Father Xavier rest in God's peace.

*   *   *

Retreat day—but only after taking part in a dialogue at Wrentham, driving back home, stopping at the hospital, attending to mail and lunch, then finally out to the hermitage.

Three of the last six weeks have been absorbed by meetings, coming and going, resulting in a breakdown of regular spiritual and ascetical practices, resulting in an emergence of my strong sensuality. I need now to get a renewed grip on myself. I find in practice I am helped by a regular schedule or plan of things; therefore I will draw up something.

Reviewing the time since my retreat, my former schedule went well. The practice of prostrations was a real blessing. I can renew my schedule:

    2:30   Rise, prostrations, wash, meditate
    3:30   Vigils, meditation, reflective reading, etc.
    6:40   Lauds, Mass, study or work
   10:00   Tierce, work

11:15	Meditation, Sext, mail
12:30	Dinner, Confessions
2:00	None, work
4:15	Meditation, *Lectio*
5:40	Vespers, supper, conference
7:40	Compline, serious reading
9:00	Prostrations, reading, Scripture text for the night
9:30	Sleep

If I find I need more sleep, I will cut down the reading after Compline.

*   *   *

Thirty-five years ago I was Confirmed, receiving the Gift without really knowing what it was all about. Now I know a little more, have received a little more, yet I am so much more conscious of sin, have so much more sin in me. All week I have been plagued by the spirit of fornication and have not been able to bring myself to declare simply and totally, "Jesus is my Lord." As I write this, the grace comes, for it is obvious that it is the only thing to do. I received the Sacrament of Reconciliation today for this. The thing I need most—at least very much—is real openness with a spiritual father. I must pray more and get more time with the Abbot. For now, Jesus is my Lord. I say that with some fear, not wanting to pay the price of perfect discipleship. O Lord, please help me to see that you are the only way, that I am fooling myself when I seek other things. Lord, help me to begin to be a monk, too busy embracing you to notice other things. Lord, my Lord, help me!

*   *   *

You do not belong to yourselves.

——1 Corinthians 6:19

Saint Paul is speaking specifically about the body here. My body does not belong to me. It is God's. He has made it his temple. He had redeemed it, bought it from slavery, the ownership of sin, self—the false self of phoniness and facade. It belongs to him. It is not enough just to keep it for him, not wasting it or giving it to another in sin. It must be used for him—in work, in adoration. It must be kept with dignity because it belongs to the Lord—cleanliness, posture, weight control, exercise. It must be cared for so it will be and remain a thing of beauty and dignity as his dwelling place: "Don't you realize that your body is a temple of the Holy Spirit, who is within you. . . . Glorify God in your body."

*　　　*　　　*

"The Holy Spirit, who is within you, *whom God has given to you*." God has really given me his Spirit. He is now *my* Spirit. The Spirit is love—divine love personified; all the love of the Father for the Son and of the Son for the Father. And now that love is mine. So I am loved. And so can I love. He is *my* Spirit and I can pour him out in love upon anyone and everyone. This is a fundamental part of the mission of every Christian—who is called to fill up what is wanting in the Passion of Christ—to pour out the Spirit, his Spirit, now my Spirit—in love, as was symbolized by the blood and water flowing out of his heart at the end of the Calvary drama. On each one I meet today I can pour out the fullness of divine Love with all his healing and affirmation. Even as I sit here I can pour out that healing and saving Love on my brothers and sisters suffering so terribly in Cambodia, Iran, Palestine, North Ireland, the slums of the Americas. This is at the heart of the contemplative vocation: a freedom from other tasks to be free to pour out Divine Love. This is why we rise in the night. This is why we are said to be at the heart of the Church. We are to be pouring out the saving, healing, renewing, vitalizing Divine Love which is ours because God has given him to us as gift: "the Holy Spirit . . . whom God has given you."

*　　　*　　　*

We seniors need to ask ourselves: Can the juniors look up to us and see encouraging models? The Rule says we should love the juniors and they are to reverence us. One of the ways we love them is by making it easier for them to reverence us. Another is to give them hope. The fact that age or infirmity requires that we be exempted from some or many things is not the problem. Old Father Bernard could do nothing but smile and pray—and he did that constantly, and we all experienced the radiance of his holiness, and were greatly encouraged. Father Owen has to eat six times a day now, but he is still a most loved model, a witness to the kind of fullness a monk can hope for. It is not the observance but the "being" and the fundamental attitude that speaks. We can't do much about "being"—that is God's doing. But maybe with him and his grace we can work on the attitude.

*   *   *

I am in a quandary about P. He is very good, open, honest, yet so easy-going. He seems to lack a self-starter. This morning he went back to bed after Vigils and slept through Lauds and Mass. When I woke him he said very simply: "God still loves me." So true. But is he meant for Trappist life here? A really strict rule is probably what he needs to keep going—but we don't keep after a person here at Spencer. The Rule is there, but each is left much on his own with the responsibility of living it in fullness. Maybe P. needs a more structured and disciplined community, one with more accountability, which would keep after him. Or maybe he needs an easier way of life, more free-flowing, for he seems comfortable flowing along, taking what comes. To commit oneself to a demanding way of life like ours and then not live up to it could be in the end very depressing and far from sanctifying.

*   *   *

Love is the fountain of life.

*

He who loves God is with God according to the measure of his love.

*

The Kingdom of God and his justice are to be sought within your own souls.

*

I wish that you would make this a general rule for yourself: that you hold suspect everyone who fears to say openly what he has whispered in your ear.

*

Value yourself above your possessions.

——Saint Bernard

* * *

I feel ill prepared for today's class. Maybe it is just the treatise we are doing. *Precepts and Dispensations* seems lacking in the fire and mystical spirit of Saint Bernard's other works. Yet it is packed with solid and challenging doctrine. If one really embraced the fullness of the way of obedience that Bernard traces out he would have a life of great peace and purity and freedom, but such total letting go is rare. It calls for great zeal for an humble way of life.

*

My first full retreat day in a long time. I did come in from the hermitage at midday to say Mass because I had a couple of appointments with students after None, but they didn't show up, so I am still retreating this evening. All is at peace and joyful, though full of desire for more and more of our good God. It is difficult to formulate any practical resolves. I will try to cut down a little more on sleep and food. I need some practical help to make community periods of prayer—mental prayer—more truly prayer. I will try letting our Lord speak to me through the Gospels for a few minutes—see if that helps—

though I would think Vigils or Vespers should give me enough.

I read today the precious chapters of John, 13–17, the core of Christian life—the outpouring of Christ's heart. If I can only more fully live them.

*　　*　　*

I am not that convinced of the value of this journal-keeping to remember it each night. I spoke to the Abbot about it today. He outlined the values and the dangers. He has tried it himself and let it go.

*　　*　　*

In prayer, what we are really ultimately looking for (unless we are fools) is Jesus/God himself. Sometimes when others ask us for something, the thing they are really looking for is the gift of *self*, with or without the other thing.

*　　*　　*

The charism of leadership is something God can give to all in the community and all should be generally encouraged to seek it. The Superior's charism is to minister to all the charisms in the community, to seek to discern the true from the false, and to coordinate all the gifts in the service of the whole.

*　　*　　*

Saint Edmund and Saint Gertrude

Today is special for me, both because of Dom Edmund and because of the grace I received three years ago at Mont-des-Cats. I am too busy and do not allow enough space for such "visits." One of the priests in the discussion on Centering Prayer yesterday emphasized that this was the kind of prayer for those who were willing to waste time on God. Wasting time on him—just sitting with him—is the way concretely we seek those precious visits of the Word. My mind is buzzing with many projects: Tapes for NCR, a volume of articles on the

Cistercian Fathers, the course for the juniors, two or three other books, an introduction for Tom's book, the retreat for Big Sur, the sermon for the Feast of Christ the King, the cottage talks ... It doesn't leave much time to waste on the Lord. I need to slow down.

*   *   *

Thanksgiving

I can be thankful that my cold has finally subsided.

And so much more. It has been a good year, a year of growth for the community and for myself. I think for the Church at large, too, under the leadership of Pope John Paul II. For the world, it is not so easy to say. A glance across the nations leaves much pain: the holocaust taking place in Cambodia, the genocide in East Timnos, the fanaticism in Iran and elsewhere in the Moslem world, the terrorism and fratricide in Ireland, the strife in Israel and Lebanon, the widespread suffering of minorities and the poor, the racial hatred in Africa and America, the frequent neglect of the old and the handicapped and the mentally ill. So much pain and suffering, frustration and anger, because we do not love one another and care for one another. So much heedless suffering we pile on ourselves. When will we all learn the ways that lead to peace and brotherhood?

Lord, have mercy. We do thank you for so much, even more than we deserve. Yet we need so much more to find our true humanity.

*   *   *

I am on the verge of losing my teeth—one of those diminishments that puts us in face of our mortality, one in that succession of diminishments that ultimately lead to the final diminishment when we put off the body itself and go forth. Standing in face of it, what sense can we make out of it? We have to turn to that one death which gives significance to all else; that one death that was the greatest—and most life-giving—event in the history of the creation. Its paradox is

summed up in the dying Man's own words: "My God, why
have you forsaken me?" and "Father, into your hands I commend my spirit." Graphically it was presented in the two men
who hung at his right and left. At first, facing death, they could
only curse it. Then one of them looked at Christ, and death
took on a new meaning—hope. It was seen as a gateway to life.
For the other who refused to turn to him and learn the
meaning of the mystery of death, there was no divine word—
only darkness and diminishment—the beginning of an eternal
death (though we can hope in God's all-embracing mercy that
he, too, made an unrecorded breakthrough). We have been
baptized into the death of Christ, and also his resurrection. We
went down into the waters—but we came up again. Keeping
our eyes on that reality, we can face each day's diminishments
with hope—each day's death is a gateway to life. Take up your
cross daily . . . Unless the grain of wheat die . . . Thy Kingdom
come!

*   *   *

Feast of Christ Our King

Some of the aspects of the liturgical changes are very
good. The idea of having a real Feast of Thanksgiving as the
year comes toward a close is very good. And now to have this
feast of Christ the King—the commemoration of the ultimate
triumph of Christ, a sort of fifteenth station. The Church year
used to end with a certain gloom; now it ends with a certain
consummation in hope and triumph. We can rejoice, for all
things are ours and we are Christ's and Christ is God's.

*

The idea of "king" is not a natural for us in America. What
then? Who is Christ for *me*? We have to give a very personal
answer to that very basic question. But a personal answer is not
enough. "King" is a social and political concept. We are not
truly disciples of Christ and who he is if we are not responding
to our social responsibilities, political obligations, and world
concerns with Christ's own reaching and concern. This is true

for monks as well as for anyone else in this world. How do we earn our living, plugging into the economic order around us? How are we responding to the crisis in Cambodia, Iran, North Ireland, etc.? We have our political obligations: voting, writing to our representatives, seeking to influence them by word as well as by our prayer. The proper use of the land we have is important—a sense of ecological well-being for the region. The alms we have received, the money we earn, the taxes we pay, all have their consequences and we have to be aware of them. The mind of Christ, our King, should guide us in all of this. Then we are truly his disciples, his followers, and we can become his sons and friends.

*

Is God redistributing the wealth of the earth? The West must decrease, and the rest of the world, the East, the South, must increase.

*

The outer limits of the age of material expansion are about to be reached, if they have not already been reached. The change this will effect on society and the way of life will be experienced most in the United States, the most materialistic culture in the world. There is great need for a return to Christian theology which recognizes the limits and the finiteness of all that is created and which teaches self-denial, sharing, and solidarity. We need to move toward an ecologically balanced state in which cooperation and sacrifice for mutual survival will be the norm. Otherwise we will see a war of all against all for the remains of a contracting economic pie.

*

Each major cause of hunger could be averted or overcome if the human community were to act cooperatively and decisively.... If hunger is indeed to be overcome, there must be a candid appreciation of its causes, a real willingness to work for the common

good of all mankind, and an authentic sharing of econ-
omies and political power among and within all nations.

——Presidential Commission on World Hunger

*

It is a time of great hope or great despair. With the
proliferation of nuclear power, either we must rise to a new
level of consciousness, one that will give us an innate sense of
our solidarity and accountability so that we will never use this
power destructively, or we surely will use the power and wipe
ourselves out and make the earth, if it survives at all, uninhab-
itable. It is an exciting, frightening time.

Never before has man stockpiled weapons and not used
them. Never before have we so needed to hear the word of the
Lord: "Choose life." Never before have we so consciously and
resolutely been doing the opposite and choosing death, in the
abortion mills, in hospitals that were consecrated to life, in the
great corporations that devour the earth for their own profits,
in the making of arms that starve the poor and leave all under
the cloud of constant threat, sapping the joy of life. How can a
man think he is working for his children when he is making
arms?

Lord, have mercy.
Thy Kingdom come!